STEP-BY-STEP
20-Minute Cookbook

STEP-BY-STEP

20-Minute Cookbook

Steven Wheeler

Photography by James Duncan

LORENZ BOOKS

First published in 1995 by Lorenz Books

© Anness Publishing Limited

Lorenz Books is an imprint of
Anness Publishing Limited
Boundary Row Studios
1 Boundary Row
London SE1 8HP

Distributed in Australia by Reed Books

ISBN 1 85967 032 6

A CIP catalogue record is available from the British Library.

Editorial Director: Joanna Lorenz
Series Editor: Lindsay Porter
Designer: Peter Laws
Photographer: James Duncan
Stylist: Madeleine Brehaut

Printed and bound in Hong Kong

CONTENTS

INTRODUCTION

With only 20 minutes on the clock, and as much energy as anyone can have at the end of a busy day, we would all like to put good food on the table with minimum fuss. Every day we wonder what miracles we can perform with the usual ingredients. Rice, pasta and potatoes, chicken, mince and pork, all continue to call for fresh inspiration. Here are 50 recipes that promise to put renewed vigour and interest back into your everyday cooking.

Recipes divide into five chapters: starters, which could also be served as light meals, fish, meat and vegetarian dishes, and desserts. Ideas are based on the use of produce that is full of colour, freshness and above all flavour. These qualities are essential to all cooking, but especially food that is prepared quickly.

Good cooking is about getting the maximum flavour from the main ingredients used. A piece of pork is good cooked plainly with simple seasoning, but throw in a few fresh sliced peaches and some soft green peppercorns and all three components will taste better and brighter. This sort of cooking is fast, intelligent and worthwhile, and is ideal for the mid-week rush. When you have a little more time to be with family and friends, a starter and/or dessert may be in order.

When one dish follows another, it is important for our comfort and digestion that they are well suited. A creamy soup does not, for instance, sit well with a rich main course. If you have the time to cook more than one course, turn to the carefully planned menus set out on pages 16–23. Preparation and cooking times vary for these menus, and some cooks will be quicker off the mark than others, but once you are familiar with a recipe, the timing will seem reasonable.

20 Minutes to Spare

Getting your act together enough to put a decent meal on the table day after day can take some doing. For many, cooking will always be a chore, while others will rise to the challenge and win. This section looks at ways to plan, shop and cook with as little effort as possible.

A lot of unnecessary running around can be prevented by sitting down with pencil and paper and drawing up a plan of action. Too often, ideas get the green light before realizing how much time and effort are

needed to produce them. The first question to ask yourself is 'How much time and energy do I have?' Be realistic – a lot of cooks come unstuck when they take on more than they can handle. Be kind to yourself and choose something you can

cope with. You'll not only enjoy preparing the meal, you might even be composed enough to sit down and enjoy it.

Cooking becomes a pleasure when we can recognize and choose the finest ingredients to work with. There is also a freedom to be had knowing which ingredients serve only to clutter our cupboards and refrigerators. Being able to see clearly what is good at a glance is one of the secrets of trouble-free cooking. Every item that

we shop for has a value associated with price, flavour and convenience. If price exceeds flavour, reconsider. If flavour is lost for the sake of convenience – powdered mashed potato, for instance – you should think again. The cook's ultimatum should be flavour and convenience at the right price.

Shopping with a nose for flavour and freshness is the best way to fight through the consumer jungle and arrive home with quality produce. Choose well and give your cooking the head start that it deserves.

The following pages show what you might find in the cupboard of a flavour-conscious cook. Sweet and savoury ingredients are best kept separate, apart from those that double up, such as flour, cornflour, sugar and eggs. Ingredients that are used frequently, such as onions, garlic, oil, wine and fruit, make an attractive and convenient display kept on the work surface. All ingredients, whether in the cupboard or not, should be used up and replaced on a regular basis. Ground spices lose their punch after around eight months, so it makes sense to replace them with fresh. Nuts also lose their freshness and can taste rancid if kept past their sell-by date. With a well-stocked cupboard of basics in peak condition, the

idea of producing a tasty meal in 20 minutes needn't present quite so many problems.

Before starting, ask yourself three questions. How much time and energy do I have? What ingredients do I have in the refrigerator? What is the quickest way I can turn time, energy and ingredients into a satisfying meal? Develop a strategy on paper that shows exactly what you are cooking, what shopping you need and where you have to go to get it. Do your shopping in one stop and try to write your list in accordance with the layout of the store. Back-tracking for the last few items on your list is no one's idea of fun.

When even the simplest meals are properly thought out,

three-quarters of the work is done. From your list you know exactly what you are cooking, what shopping you need, where to get it and what you are going to do with the ingredients when you start to get to work in the kitchen.

It's always worth taking a few minutes to read a recipe through before you start. This should enable you to have all the necessary equipment to hand from the outset. It has to be said that some cooks are more organized in their kitchens than others. Some cooks clean and tidy up with near-surgical precision, while others thrive in varying degrees of chaos. Cooking quickly

depends on: a) knowing what you are doing, and b) being able to put your hands on what you need as you go. Most cooks work best of all in a relatively creative mess where somehow everything comes together in the end. Whatever conditions you are comfortable with, make sure they are 'just so' before you begin cooking.

Store Cupboard Ingredients

The following ingredients are shown left to right from the top shelf.

Polenta
Italian cornmeal. Serve with Gorgonzola cheese and salad.

Flour
All-purpose and self-raising flour are used for making white sauces and pancakes.

Lentils
Red lentils soften quickly for simple soups and sauces.

Couscous
Cracked wheat for tabbouleh-style salads.

Sesame seeds
Nutty and rich when toasted.

Spices
Cumin, coriander, fennel seed, cardamom and peppercorns are best when freshly ground.

Pasta
Use best quality fine vermicelli for soups, and spaghetti and other pasta shapes with sauces.

Wild mushrooms
Deeply flavoured dried ceps and morels come alive in hot water.

Fresh herbs
Parsley, thyme, garlic and rosemary add instant flavour.

Long-grain and risotto rice
Use white easy-cook rice as it has a good flavour.

Almonds
These provide a rich flavour in sauces and salsas.

Buckwheat
Robustly flavoured grain. Cook with couscous.

Garlic in oil
Garlic cloves keep their flavour in olive oil (see page 14).

Tarragon in vinegar
Keep fresh tarragon in wine vinegar for year-round flavour.

Pine nuts
The intensely rich fruit of the pine cone. A great asset to vegetarian dishes.

Stock cubes
Good quality stock cubes are indispensable. Buy the additive-free type if you can.

Cornflour
This is used for thickening sauces and gravies.

Capers
The fairly sharp taste of capers makes an ideal accompaniment to meat dishes.

Mustard
A piquant addition to meats and savoury sauces.

Green peppercorns
Soft berries with an assertive heat. Delicious with pork.

Pesto sauce
Made from basil, garlic, pine nuts, cheese and olive oil. Use for speedy pasta dishes.

Pasta sauce
Make your own from a can of tomatoes (see page 15). Serve with an Italian hard cheese.

Canned vegetables
Young vegetables are easy to serve with grilled meat and fish.

Citrus fruits
Bright oranges, lemons and limes offer fresh fruit flavours to savoury cooking.

Onions
Onions, like garlic and root ginger, add delicious flavour to a variety of dishes.

Wine
Sober judgment allows a measure of wine, as and when it pleases the cook!

Oils
Keep olive oil for flavour, and a variety such as groundnut for neutral taste.

Vinegar
Use a good white wine vinegar. Balsamic vinegar should be used only sparingly.

Olives and pickled peppers
These will provide a taste of the sun in the winter.

Eggs
Fast-food convenience in a shell. Properly fed hens lay the best and tastiest eggs.

Dessert Store Cupboard Ingredients

The following ingredients are shown left to right from the centre shelf.

Flour
Plain and self-raising flour can be used for fast sponges, tarts and easy pancakes.

Caster sugar
This is a free-flow, fast-mix, easy-blend sugar suited to all good cakes and bakes.

Icing sugar
This is powder-fine for easy icing and dusting. Sift before using to remove any lumps.

Meringues
Store-bought meringues kept in an airtight jar can be used for impromptu puddings.

Chocolate sauce
Make your own (see page 15). Delicious with ice cream, sprinkled with toasted nuts.

Cocoa powder
Use sugarless cocoa powder in drinks and desserts for a rich chocolate taste.

Chocolate
Buy the best quality chocolate you can afford and store it at room temperature, never in the refrigerator.

Cornflour
Use this combined half-and-half with flour for fine textured cakes and sponges.

Citrus fruits
Oranges, lemons and limes offer zestful flavour. Heavy fruits offer the juiciest squeeze.

Cherries
Enjoy these fresh in season, as they have a poor flavour when cooked. Choose sour, or buy ready-bottled for cooking.

Melon
Fill your kitchen with the scent of a ripe melon. Serve cold with red berry fruit when in season.

Bananas
Bananas are deliciously sweet when speckled brown.

Pineapple
Pineapples are ripe when the skin smells sweet.

Strawberries
Traditionally served with sugar and cream, but also ideal for use in hot and cold puddings, cakes and tarts.

Pears
Partner pears with Parmesan, pecorino, Gorgonzola or Roquefort cheeses.

Apples
Red, green and russet skins conceal a host of flavour. All these apples make a juicy and crisp addition to quick desserts.

Peaches
Remove the skins from sun-ripened peaches by plunging in boiling water.

Passion fruit
The sour, scented juice of this fruit is delicious when combined with strawberries and raspberries.

Grapes
There are innumerable varieties of grapes available, and they can be red, green or seedless. Muscat grapes offer the best flavour and sweetness.

Finger wafers
These and other ice cream accessories are a must for spur-of-the-moment desserts.

Brown sugar
Less refined than white, brown sugars are rich in molasses. Dark sugars are stronger in taste.

Flaked almonds
Uninteresting raw, a temptation when toasted. Scatter over ice cream, chocolate and summer fruit for the finishing touch.

Ground almonds
Essential for moist cakes and sponges; substitute half flour with ground almonds in any baking recipe.

Preserved fruit
Use canned or bottled apricots and raspberries for easy convenience in desserts.

Eggs
Store and use eggs at room temperature.

Salad Dressing Baste

A good salad dressing can double up as an effective baste for the grill and barbecue. This dressing is delicious with white meats as well as fish.

Makes 105 ml/7 tbsp

INGREDIENTS
90 ml/6 tbsp olive oil
15 ml/1 tbsp white wine vinegar
5 ml/1 tsp French mustard
½ garlic clove, crushed
1 ml/¼ tsp sugar

1 Pour the oil and vinegar into a screw-topped jar.

2 Add the mustard, garlic and sugar.

3 Shake well, and use as a dressing or marinade for salad, meat and fish.

Garlic Oil

To capture the freshness of garlic, keep crushed cloves in olive oil and use in dressings, sauces and for cooking.

Makes 120 ml/4 fl oz/ ½ cup

INGREDIENTS
6–8 garlic cloves
120 ml/4 fl oz/½ cup olive oil

1 Trim the root end from 6–8 cloves of garlic. Tap each clove sharply under the side of a large knife, banging with a fist until the clove splits and the skin loosens. Discard the skin.

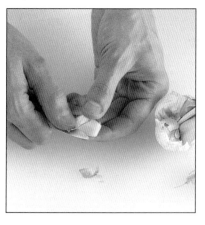

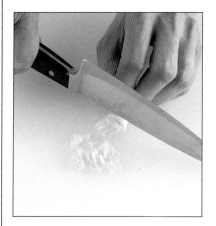

2 Use the back of a heavy knife, near the handle, to crush the garlic. Hold firmly with the end of the blade resting on the chopping board, secure the clove with your thumb and forefinger, then crush with a chopping motion.

3 Transfer the crushed garlic into a screw-topped jar, cover with olive oil and store at room temperature. The oil will keep for up to six weeks.

COOK'S TIP

Garlic and other substances are not preserved in oil, and there is concern that bacteria may form if kept too long. Do not keep the oil for longer than two weeks. If kept in the refrigerator the oil may solidify, but can be used if left to soften at room temperature.

Pasta Sauce

Keep this easy sauce in mind when you want a tomato topping for pasta.

Makes 750 ml/1¼ pints/3⅔ cups

INGREDIENTS
2 × 400 g/14 oz cans chopped
    tomatoes
60 ml/4 tbsp olive oil
2 garlic cloves, crushed
10 ml/2 tsp fresh thyme
10 ml/2 tsp anchovy essence
    (optional)
2.5 ml/½ tsp black olive paste
    (optional)
2.5 ml/½ tsp freshly ground black
    pepper

1 Empty the tomatoes into a nylon sieve set over a bowl. The juices will run clear after a short time. Allow the tomatoes to thicken for 10 minutes.

2 Heat the oil and garlic in a saucepan and add the thyme, sieved tomatoes, anchovy essence and olive paste, if using. Simmer for 5 minutes, then season to taste with black pepper. Liquidize in a blender if you like a smooth sauce.

3 If you are not using the sauce immediately, spoon into a preserving jar. This sauce will keep refrigerated for up to seven days.

Chocolate Sauce

Every cook should have a jar of chocolate sauce to hand for last minute dessert making. Serve hot or cold over ice cream, steamed puddings and pastries.

Makes 225 ml/8 fl oz/1 cup

INGREDIENTS
150 ml/¼ pint/⅔ cup single cream
15 ml/1 tbsp caster sugar
150 g/5 oz best quality plain
    chocolate, broken
30 ml/2 tbsp dark rum or whisky
    (optional)

1 Rinse out a small saucepan with cold water to prevent the sauce from catching. Bring the cream and sugar to the boil.

2 Remove from the heat, add the chocolate and stir until melted. Stir in the alcohol, if using.

3 Pour the chocolate sauce into a closed jar. When cool, refrigerate for up to ten days. Reheat by standing the jar in a saucepan of simmering water, or microwave on high power (100%) for 2 minutes and stir.

Menu Planner

All of the recipes in this book can be prepared individually in 20 minutes or less, but they can all be combined with other dishes to provide a three-course meal. Below are some suggested menus, explaining how to co-ordinate the preparation and cooking times required, so that you can prepare two or more courses simultaneously. To follow the menus, work across each row, from left to right, and then down the chart to the end. Some quick starter and dessert ideas have been included, which require very little preparation.

MENU 1

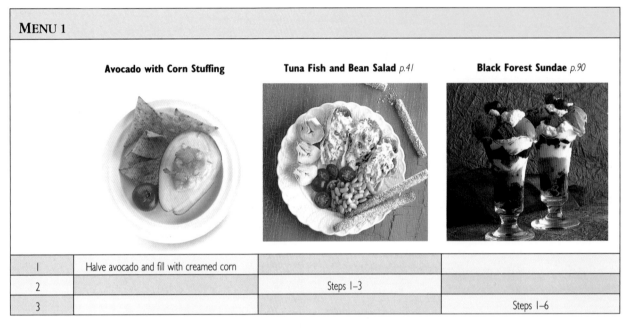

		Avocado with Corn Stuffing	Tuna Fish and Bean Salad p.41	Black Forest Sundae p.90
1		Halve avocado and fill with creamed corn		
2			Steps 1–3	
3				Steps 1–6

MENU 2

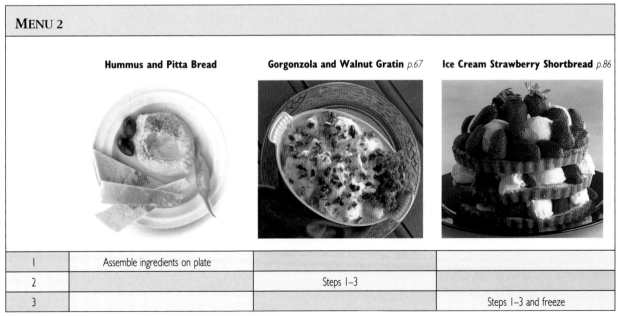

		Hummus and Pitta Bread	Gorgonzola and Walnut Gratin p.67	Ice Cream Strawberry Shortbread p.86
1		Assemble ingredients on plate		
2			Steps 1–3	
3				Steps 1–3 and freeze

MENU 3

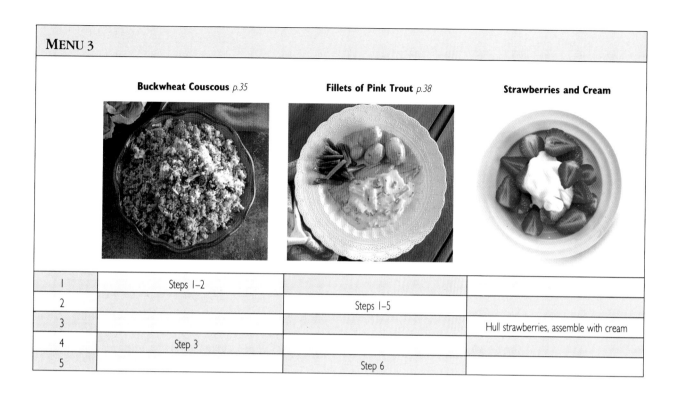

Buckwheat Couscous *p.35* **Fillets of Pink Trout** *p.38* **Strawberries and Cream**

	Buckwheat Couscous	Fillets of Pink Trout	Strawberries and Cream
1	Steps 1–2		
2		Steps 1–5	
3			Hull strawberries, assemble with cream
4	Step 3		
5		Step 6	

MENU 4

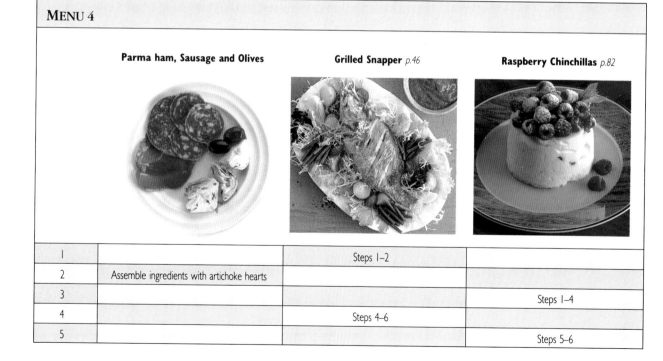

Parma ham, Sausage and Olives **Grilled Snapper** *p.46* **Raspberry Chinchillas** *p.82*

	Parma ham, Sausage and Olives	Grilled Snapper	Raspberry Chinchillas
1		Steps 1–2	
2	Assemble ingredients with artichoke hearts		
3			Steps 1–4
4		Steps 4–6	
5			Steps 5–6

MENU 5

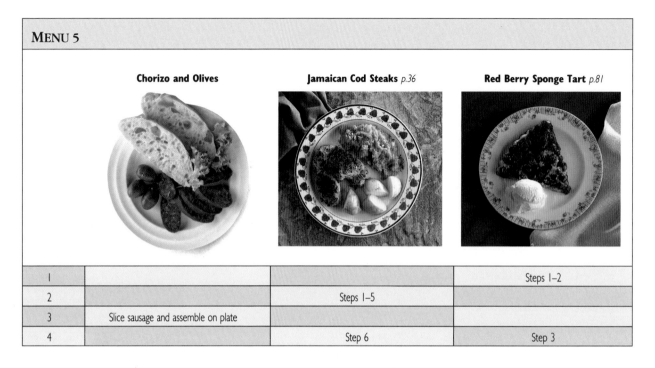

Chorizo and Olives   **Jamaican Cod Steaks** *p.36*   **Red Berry Sponge Tart** *p.81*

	Chorizo and Olives	Jamaican Cod Steaks	Red Berry Sponge Tart
1			Steps 1–2
2		Steps 1–5	
3	Slice sausage and assemble on plate		
4		Step 6	Step 3

MENU 6

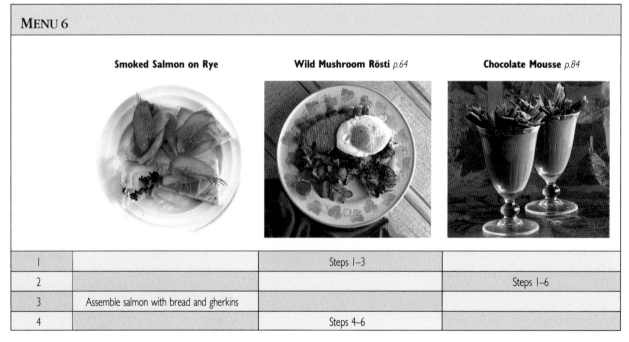

Smoked Salmon on Rye   **Wild Mushroom Rösti** *p.64*   **Chocolate Mousse** *p.84*

	Smoked Salmon on Rye	Wild Mushroom Rösti	Chocolate Mousse
1		Steps 1–3	
2			Steps 1–6
3	Assemble salmon with bread and gherkins		
4		Steps 4–6	

MENU 7

	Beetroot and Butter Bean Soup *p.28*	Macaroni Cheese with Mushrooms *p.73*	Pineapple, Strawberries and Sorbet

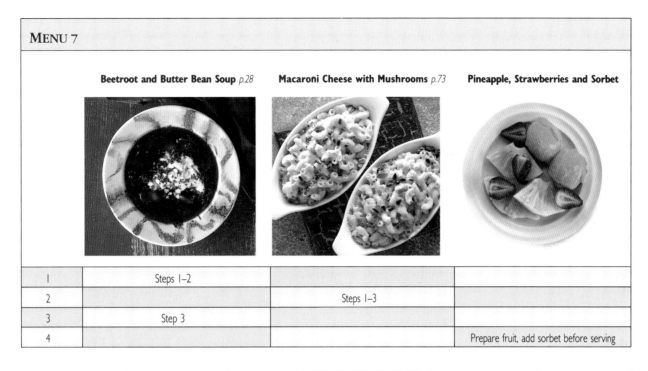

1	Steps 1–2		
2		Steps 1–3	
3	Step 3		
4			Prepare fruit, add sorbet before serving

MENU 8

	Baby Carrot and Fennel Soup *p.29*	Sausage Popovers *p.62*	Melon and Berries

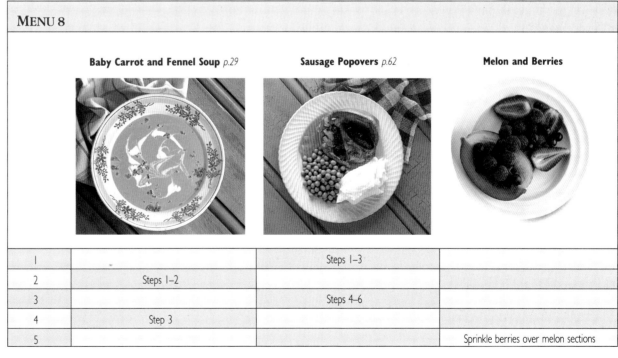

1		Steps 1–3	
2	Steps 1–2		
3		Steps 4–6	
4	Step 3		
5			Sprinkle berries over melon sections

MENU 9

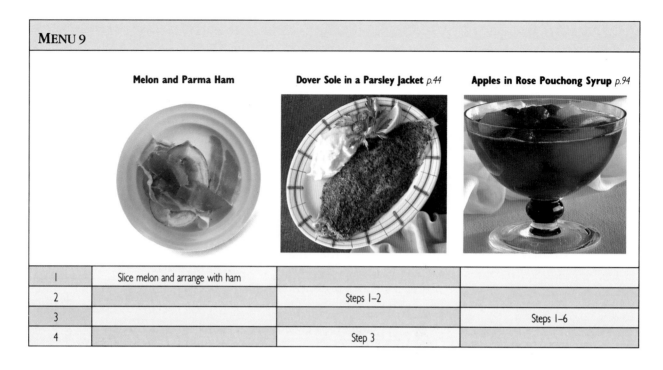

			Melon and Parma Ham	Dover Sole in a Parsley Jacket *p.44*	Apples in Rose Pouchong Syrup *p.94*
1	Slice melon and arrange with ham		
2		Steps 1–2	
3			Steps 1–6
4		Step 3	

MENU 10

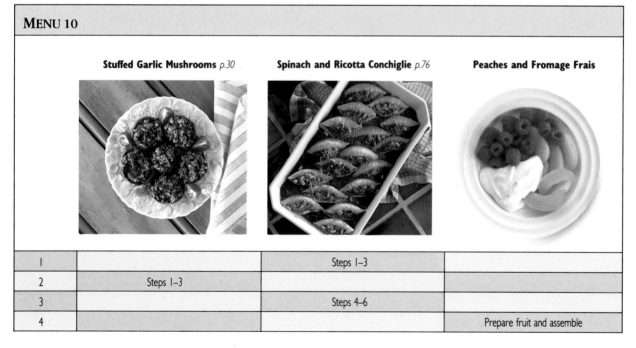

	Stuffed Garlic Mushrooms *p.30*	Spinach and Ricotta Conchiglie *p.76*	Peaches and Fromage Frais
1		Steps 1–3	
2	Steps 1–3		
3		Steps 4–6	
4			Prepare fruit and assemble

MENU 11

Welsh Rarebit Toasts *p.34* **Succotash Soup Plate** *p.79* **Melon and Raspberries**

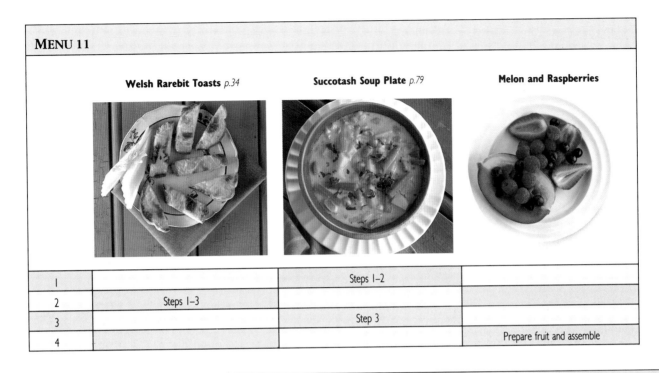

	Welsh Rarebit Toasts	Succotash Soup Plate	Melon and Raspberries
1		Steps 1–2	
2	Steps 1–3		
3		Step 3	
4			Prepare fruit and assemble

MENU 12

Crab and Egg Noodle Broth *p.26* **Indonesian Pork and Peanut Saté** *p.59* **Tropical Fruit Salad**

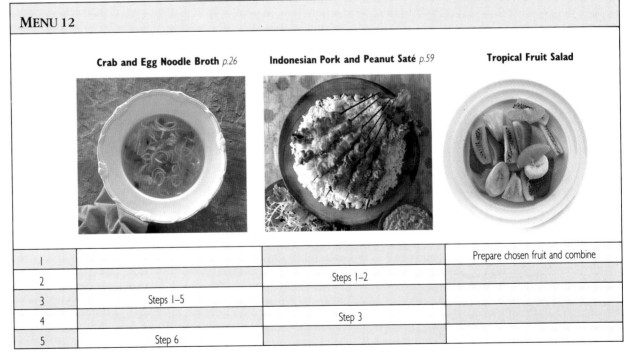

	Crab and Egg Noodle Broth	Indonesian Pork and Peanut Saté	Tropical Fruit Salad
1			Prepare chosen fruit and combine
2		Steps 1–2	
3	Steps 1–5		
4		Step 3	
5	Step 6		

MENU 13

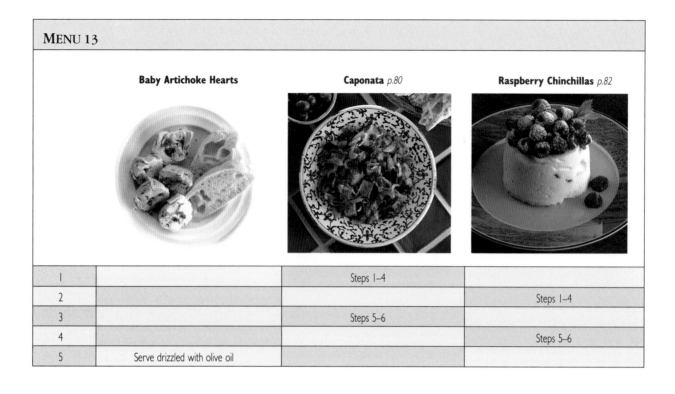

Baby Artichoke Hearts   **Caponata** *p.80*   **Raspberry Chinchillas** *p.82*

	Baby Artichoke Hearts	Caponata	Raspberry Chinchillas
1		Steps 1–4	
2			Steps 1–4
3		Steps 5–6	
4			Steps 5–6
5	Serve drizzled with olive oil		

MENU 14

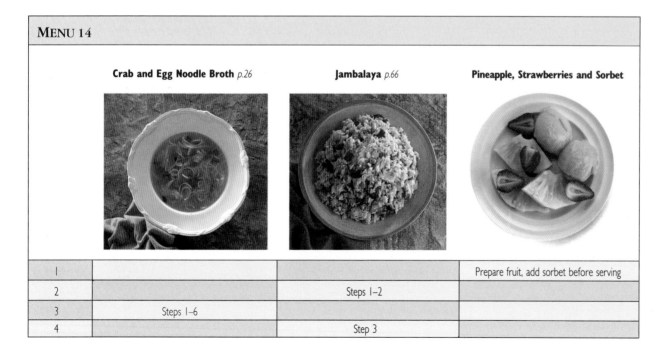

Crab and Egg Noodle Broth *p.26*   **Jambalaya** *p.66*   **Pineapple, Strawberries and Sorbet**

	Crab and Egg Noodle Broth	Jambalaya	Pineapple, Strawberries and Sorbet
1			Prepare fruit, add sorbet before serving
2		Steps 1–2	
3	Steps 1–6		
4		Step 3	

MENU 15

	Baby Vegetables and Dip	Pickled Herrings with Beetroot p.40	Apricot and Almond Bake p.88

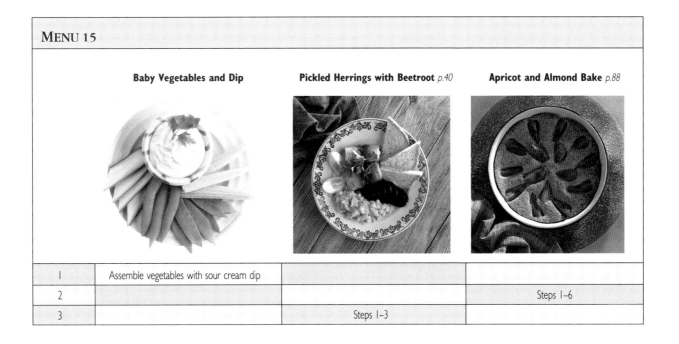

1	Assemble vegetables with sour cream dip		
2			Steps 1–6
3		Steps 1–3	

MENU 16

	Stuffed Garlic Mushrooms p.30	Spanish Omelette p.70	Fresh Figs, Chocolate and Liqueur

1	Steps 1–3		
2		Steps 1–6	
3			Fill figs with chocolate and drizzle with liqueur

Fresh Pea and Ham Soup

Frozen peas provide flavour, freshness and colour in this delicious winter soup, which is filling enough to make a light main course or a starter.

Serves 4

INGREDIENTS

115 g/4 oz small pasta shapes
30 ml/2 tbsp vegetable oil
1 small bunch spring onions, chopped
350 g/12 oz/3 cups frozen peas
1.2 litres/2 pints/5 cups chicken stock
225 g/8 oz raw unsmoked ham
   or gammon
60 ml/4 tbsp double cream
salt and freshly ground black pepper
warm crusty bread, to serve

PREPARATION TIME

10 minutes

COOKING TIME

10 minutes

ham

pasta

cream

peas

spring onions

1 Bring a large saucepan of salted water to the boil. Toss in the pasta and cook according to the instructions on the packet. Drain, cover with cold water and set aside until required.

2 Heat the vegetable oil in a large heavy saucepan and cook the spring onions until soft. Add the peas and stock, then simmer for 10 minutes.

3 Liquidize the soup in a blender and return to the saucepan. Cut the ham or gammon into short fingers and add it together with the pasta to the saucepan. Simmer for 2–3 minutes and season to taste. Stir in the cream and serve with the warm crusty bread.

VARIATION

Any pasta shapes can be used for this soup, although hoops or shells seem to work best of all.

French Onion Soup

In the time it takes to soften a few onions and brown some cheese on toast, this delicious soup appears on the table steaming hot and ready to eat. It makes a substantial starter or lunch dish.

Serves 4

INGREDIENTS
30 ml/2 tbsp vegetable oil
3 medium onions, sliced
900 ml/1 ½ pints/3¾ cups beef stock
4 slices French bread
butter, for spreading
115 g/4 oz/1 cup grated Gruyère,
   or Emmenthal cheese

PREPARATION TIME
10 minutes

COOKING TIME
10 minutes

onions

cheese

French bread

1 Heat the vegetable oil in a large frying pan and brown the onions over a steady heat, taking care they do not burn.

2 Transfer the browned onions to a large saucepan, cover with beef stock and simmer for 10 minutes.

3 Preheat the grill to a moderate temperature and toast the French bread on both sides. Spread one side with butter and top with grated cheese. Ladle the soup into four flameproof dishes, float the cheesy crusts on top and grill until crispy and brown.

COOK'S TIP
The flavour and richness of French onion soup will improve if the soup is kept chilled in the refrigerator for three to four days.

Crab and Egg Noodle Broth

This delicious broth is an ideal solution when you are hungry and time is short, and you need something fast, nutritious and filling.

Serves 4

INGREDIENTS
75 g/3 oz fine egg noodles
25 g/1 oz/2 tbsp unsalted butter
1 small bunch spring onions, chopped
1 celery stick, sliced
1 medium carrot, peeled and cut
    into batons
1.2 litres/2 pints/5 cups chicken stock
60 ml/4 tbsp dry sherry
115 g/4 oz white crab meat, fresh
    or frozen
pinch of celery salt
pinch of cayenne pepper
10 ml/2 tsp lemon juice
1 small bunch coriander or flat-leaf
    parsley, to garnish

PREPARATION AND COOKING TIME

20 minutes

celery

egg noodles

crab meat

spring onions

coriander

COOK'S TIP
Fresh or frozen crab meat has the best flavour. Avoid canned crab, as this tastes rather bland.

1 Bring a large saucepan of salted water to the boil. Toss in the egg noodles and cook according to the instructions on the packet. Cool under cold running water and leave immersed in water until required.

2 Heat the butter in another large pan, add the spring onions, celery and carrot, cover and soften the vegetables over a gentle heat for 3–4 minutes.

3 Add the chicken stock and sherry, bring to the boil and simmer for a further 5 minutes.

4 Flake the crab meat between your fingers onto a plate and remove any stray pieces of shell.

5 Drain the noodles and add to the broth together with the crab meat. Season to taste with celery salt and cayenne pepper, and sharpen with the lemon juice. Return to a simmer.

6 Ladle the broth into shallow soup plates, scatter with roughly chopped coriander or parsley and serve.

Beetroot and Butter Bean Soup

This soup is a simplified version of borscht, and is prepared in a fraction of the time. Serve with a spoonful of sour cream and a scattering of chopped fresh parsley.

Serves 4

INGREDIENTS
30 ml/2 tbsp vegetable oil
1 medium onion, halved and sliced
5 ml/1 tsp caraway seeds
finely grated zest of ½ orange
250 g/9 oz cooked beetroot, grated
1.2 litres/2 pints/5 cups beef stock
 or rassol
1 × 400 g/14 oz can butter beans,
 drained
15 ml/1 tbsp wine vinegar
60 ml/4 tbsp sour cream
60 ml/4 tbsp chopped fresh parsley,
 to garnish

PREPARATION AND COOKING TIME

20 minutes

caraway seeds

beetroot

sour cream

onion

orange

butter beans

1 Heat the oil in a large saucepan and cook the onion, caraway seeds and orange zest until soft but not coloured.

2 Add the beetroot, stock or rassol, butter beans and vinegar and simmer for a further 10 minutes.

3 Divide the soup between four bowls, add a spoonful of sour cream to each and scatter with chopped fresh parsley.

COOK'S TIP

Rassol is a beetroot broth used to impart a strong beetroot colour and flavour. You are most likely to find it in Kosher food stores.

Baby Carrot and Fennel Soup

Sweet tender carrots find their moment of glory in this delicately spiced soup. Fennel provides an aniseed flavour without overpowering the carrots.

Serves 4

INGREDIENTS
50 g/2 oz/4 tbsp butter
1 small bunch spring onions, chopped
150 g/5 oz fennel bulb, chopped
1 celery stick, chopped
450 g/1 lb new carrots, grated
2.5 ml/½ tsp ground cumin
150 g/5 oz new potatoes, peeled and diced
1.2 litres/2 pints/5 cups chicken or vegetable stock
60 ml/4 tbsp double cream
salt and freshly ground black pepper
60 ml/4 tbsp chopped fresh parsley, to garnish

PREPARATION TIME
5 minutes

COOKING TIME
15 minutes

carrots
fennel bulb
celery
cream
spring onions

1 Melt the butter in a large saucepan and add the spring onions, fennel, celery, carrots and cumin. Cover and cook for 5 minutes until soft.

2 Add the potatoes and stock, and simmer for a further 10 minutes.

3 Liquidize the mixture in the pan with a hand-held blender. Stir in the cream and season to taste. Serve in individual bowls and garnish with chopped fresh parsley.

COOK'S TIP
For convenience, you can freeze the soup in portions before adding the cream, seasoning and parsley.

Stuffed Garlic Mushrooms with a Parsley Crust

These garlic mushrooms are perfect for dinner parties, or you could serve them in larger portions as a light supper dish with a green salad. Try them stuffed with a healthy dose of freshly chopped parsley.

Serves 4

INGREDIENTS
350 g/12 oz large mushrooms, stems removed
3 garlic cloves, crushed
175 g/6 oz/¾ cup butter, softened
50 g/2 oz/1 cup fresh white breadcrumbs
50 g/2 oz/1 cup fresh parsley, chopped
1 egg, beaten
salt and cayenne pepper
8 cherry tomatoes, to garnish

PREPARATION TIME
10 minutes

COOKING TIME
10 minutes

parsley

butter   *egg*

garlic

mushrooms

breadcrumbs

1 Preheat the oven to 190°C/375°F/ Gas 5. Arrange the mushrooms cup side uppermost on a baking tray. Mix together the crushed garlic and butter in a small bowl and divide 115 g/4 oz/½ cup of the butter between the mushrooms.

2 Heat the remaining butter in a frying pan and lightly fry the breadcrumbs until golden brown. Place the chopped parsley in a bowl, add the breadcrumbs, season to taste and mix well.

3 Stir in the egg and use the mixture to fill the mushroom caps. Bake for 10–15 minutes until the topping has browned and the mushrooms have softened. Garnish with quartered tomatoes.

COOK'S TIP
If you are planning ahead, stuffed mushrooms can be prepared up to 12 hours in advance and kept in the fridge before baking.

Smoked Trout and Horseradish Salad

Salads are the easy answer to fast, healthy eating. When lettuce is sweet and crisp, partner it with fillets of smoked trout, warm new potatoes and a creamy horseradish dressing.

Serves 4

INGREDIENTS
675 g/1½ lb new potatoes
4 smoked trout fillets
115 g/4 oz mixed lettuce leaves
4 slices dark rye bread, cut into
    fingers
salt and freshly ground black pepper

FOR THE DRESSING
60 ml/4 tbsp creamed horseradish
60 ml/4 tbsp groundnut oil
15 ml/1 tbsp white wine vinegar
10 ml/2 tsp caraway seeds

PREPARATION AND COOKING TIME

20 minutes

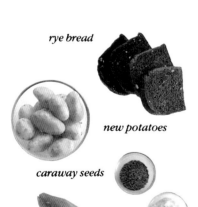

rye bread

new potatoes

caraway seeds

horseradish

smoked trout fillets

lettuce leaves

1 Bring the potatoes to the boil in a saucepan of salted water and simmer for 20 minutes. Remove the skin from the trout, and lift the flesh from the bone.

2 To make the dressing, place all the ingredients in a screw-topped jar and shake vigorously. Season the lettuce leaves and moisten them with the prepared dressing. Distribute between four plates.

3 Flake the trout fillets and halve the potatoes. Scatter them together with the rye fingers over the salad leaves and toss to mix. Season to taste and serve.

COOK'S TIP

To save time washing lettuce leaves, buy them ready-prepared from your supermarket. It is better to season the leaves rather than the dressing when making a salad.

Smoked Salmon Pancakes with Pesto and Pine Nuts

These simple pancakes take no more than 10–15 minutes to prepare and are perfect for a special occasion. Smoked salmon is delicious with fresh basil and combines well with toasted pine nuts and a spoonful of crème fraîche.

Makes 12–16

INGREDIENTS
120 ml/4 fl oz/½ cup milk
115 g/4 oz/1 cup self-raising flour
1 egg
30 ml/2 tbsp pesto sauce
vegetable oil, for frying
200 ml/7 fl oz/scant 1 cup crème fraîche
75 g/3 oz smoked salmon
15 g/½ oz/1 tbsp pine nuts, toasted
salt and freshly ground black pepper
12–16 fresh basil sprigs, to garnish

PREPARATION TIME
10 minutes

COOKING TIME
10 minutes

basil

pine nuts

crème fraîche

flour

pesto sauce

smoked salmon

1 Pour half of the milk into a mixing bowl. Add the flour, egg, pesto sauce and seasoning and mix to a smooth batter.

2 Add the remainder of the milk and stir until evenly blended.

3 Heat the vegetable oil in a large frying pan. Spoon the pancake mixture into the heated oil in small heaps. Allow about 30 seconds for the pancakes to rise, then turn and cook briefly on the other side. Continue cooking the pancakes in batches until all the batter is used up.

4 Arrange the pancakes on a serving plate and top each one with a spoonful of crème fraîche.

5 Cut the salmon into 1 cm/½ in strips and place on top of each pancake.

COOK'S TIP
If not serving immediately, cover the pancakes with a dish towel and keep warm in an oven preheated to 140°C/275°F/Gas 1.

6 Scatter each pancake with pine nuts and garnish with a sprig of fresh basil.

Welsh Rarebit Toasts

Welsh Rarebit is the gourmet's answer to cheese on toast. Serve as a tasty starter with drinks.

Serves 4

INGREDIENTS
200 ml/7 fl oz/scant 1 cup lager
60 ml/4 tbsp plain flour
10 ml/2 tsp mustard (powdered or ready-made)
2.5 ml/½ tsp celery salt
pinch of cayenne pepper
175 g/6 oz/1½ cups grated Cheddar cheese
6 thick slices white or wholemeal bread
3 celery sticks, to serve

PREPARATION TIME
15 minutes

COOKING TIME
5 minutes

bread

Cheddar cheese

flour

mustard

lager

1 Measure 50 ml/2 fl oz/¼ cup of the lager into a mixing bowl and combine with the flour, mustard, celery salt and cayenne pepper.

2 Bring the remaining lager to the boil in a heavy saucepan together with the cheese. Pour over the mixed ingredients and stir to blend evenly. Return to the saucepan and simmer gently, stirring continuously, to thicken.

3 Preheat a moderate grill and toast the bread on both sides. Spread thickly with the mixture, then grill until golden brown and bubbly. Cut into fingers and serve with celery sticks.

COOK'S TIP
Welsh Rarebit mixture will keep in the refrigerator for up to a week and is perfect for a fast snack at any time of the day.

Buckwheat Couscous with Goat's Cheese and Celery

Couscous is made from cracked, partially cooked wheat, which is dried and then reconstituted in water or stock. It tastes of very little by itself, but carries the flavour of other ingredients very well.

Serves 4

INGREDIENTS

1 egg
30 ml/2 tbsp olive oil
1 small bunch spring onions, chopped
2 celery sticks, sliced
175 g/6 oz/1 cup couscous
75 g/3 oz/½ cup buckwheat
45 ml/3 tbsp chopped fresh parsley
finely grated zest of ½ lemon
25 g/1 oz/¼ cup chopped walnuts, toasted
150 g/5 oz strongly flavoured goat's cheese
salt and freshly ground black pepper
Cos lettuce leaves, to serve

PREPARATION TIME

5 minutes

COOKING TIME

15 minutes

buckwheat

celery

egg

goat's cheese

parsley

walnuts

1 Boil the egg for 10 minutes, cool, peel and set aside. Heat the oil in a saucepan and add the spring onions and celery. Cook for 2–3 minutes until soft.

2 Add the couscous and buckwheat and cover with 600 ml/1 pint/2½ cups of boiling salted water. Cover and return to a simmer. Remove from the heat and allow the couscous to soften and absorb the water for about 3 minutes. Transfer the mixture to a large bowl.

3 Grate the hard-boiled egg finely into a small bowl and add the chopped parsley, lemon zest and walnuts. Fold into the couscous, season, and crumble in the goat's cheese. Mix well and then turn out into a shallow dish. Serve warm with a salad of Cos lettuce.

VARIATION

Couscous is ideal as a filling for pitta breads when accompanied with crisp salad leaves.

Jamaican Spiced Cod Steaks with Pumpkin Ragout

Spicy hot from Kingston town, this fast fish dish is guaranteed to appeal. The term 'ragout' is taken from the old French verb *ragouter*, which means to stimulate the appetite.

Serves 4

INGREDIENTS
finely grated zest of ½ orange
30 ml/2 tbsp black peppercorns
15 ml/1 tbsp allspice berries or
    Jamaican pepper
2.5 ml/½ tsp salt
4 × 175 g/6 oz cod steaks
groundnut oil, for frying
new potatoes, to serve (optional)
45 ml/3 tbsp chopped fresh parsley,
    to garnish

FOR THE RAGOUT
30 ml/2 tbsp groundnut oil
1 medium onion, chopped
2.5 cm/1 in fresh root ginger, peeled
    and grated
450 g/1 lb fresh pumpkin, peeled,
    deseeded and chopped
3–4 shakes of Tabasco sauce
30 ml/2 tbsp soft brown sugar
15 ml/1 tbsp vinegar

PREPARATION AND COOKING TIME

20 minutes

pumpkin

cod steaks

ginger

1 To make the ragout, heat the oil in a heavy saucepan and add the onion and ginger. Cover and cook, stirring, for 3–4 minutes until soft.

2 Add the chopped pumpkin, Tabasco sauce, brown sugar and vinegar, cover and cook over a low heat for 10–12 minutes until softened.

3 Combine the orange zest, pepper-corns, allspice or Jamaican pepper and salt, then crush coarsely using a pestle and mortar. (Alternatively, coarsely grind the peppercorns in a pepper mill and combine with the zest and seasoning.)

4 Scatter the spice mixture over both sides of the fish and moisten with a sprinkling of oil.

5 Heat a large frying pan and fry the cod steaks for 12 minutes, turning once.

6 Serve the cod steaks with a spoonful of pumpkin ragout and new potatoes, if desired, and garnish the ragout with chopped fresh parsley.

Fillets of Pink Trout with Tarragon Cream Sauce

If you do not like the idea of cooking and serving trout on the bone, ask your fishmonger to fillet and skin the fish. Serve two fillets per person.

Serves 4

INGREDIENTS
25 g/1 oz/2 tbsp butter
4 fresh trout, filleted and skinned
salt and freshly ground black pepper
new potatoes, to serve
runner beans, to serve

FOR THE CREAM SAUCE
2 large spring onions, white part
  only, chopped
½ cucumber, peeled, deseeded and
  cut into short batons
5 ml/1 tsp cornflour
150 ml/¼ pint/⅔ cup single cream
50 ml/2 fl oz/¼ cup dry sherry
30 ml/2 tbsp chopped fresh tarragon
1 tomato, chopped and deseeded

PREPARATION AND COOKING TIME
20 minutes

tomato

cucumber

spring onions

trout

cream

tarragon

VARIATION
This recipe can also be made with salmon fillets and the dry sherry may be substituted with white wine.

1 Melt the butter in a large frying pan, season the fillets and cook for 6 minutes, turning once. Transfer to a plate, cover and keep warm.

2 To make the sauce, add the spring onions and cucumber to the pan, and cook over a gentle heat, stirring, until soft but not coloured.

3 Remove the pan from the heat and stir in the cornflour.

4 Return to the heat and pour in the cream and sherry. Simmer to thicken, stirring continuously.

5 Add the chopped tarragon and tomato, and season to taste.

6 Spoon the sauce over the fillets and serve with buttered new potatoes and runner beans.

Pickled Herrings with Beetroot and Apple Relish

Soused or pickled herrings are delicious with cooked beetroot. Serve with buttered rye bread and a sweet and sour apple relish.

Serves 4

INGREDIENTS
2 eggs
8 pickled herrings
250 g/9 oz cooked baby beetroot
fresh flat-leaf parsley, to garnish
4 slices buttered rye bread, to serve
150 ml/¼ pint/⅔ cup sour cream, to serve (optional)

FOR THE RELISH
30 ml/2 tbsp vegetable oil
2 large eating apples, peeled, cored and finely chopped
1 medium onion, chopped
15 ml/1 tbsp sugar
15 ml/1 tbsp cider vinegar
5 ml/1 tsp hot mustard
pinch of salt

PREPARATION TIME
15 minutes

COOKING TIME
5 minutes

pickled herrings **eggs**

baby beetroot

onion **apples**

1 Bring a saucepan of water to the boil, gently lower in the eggs and cook for 10 minutes. Cool under running water and peel. Cut into quarters.

2 To make the relish, heat the oil in a saucepan and add the apple and onion. Cook over a gentle heat for 3–4 minutes without colouring. Add the sugar, vinegar and mustard, then season with salt.

3 Divide the herrings between four plates. Slice the beetroot and arrange to one side with the relish. Decorate with egg quarters and garnish with parsley. Serve with buttered rye bread, and a spoonful of sour cream if you wish.

COOK'S TIP
Choose full-flavoured green or red apples for the best results.

Tuna Fish and Flageolet Bean Salad

Two cans of tuna fish form the basis of this delicious store cupboard salad.

Serves 4

INGREDIENTS
90 ml/6 tbsp mayonnaise
5 ml/1 tsp mustard
30 ml/2 tbsp capers
45 ml/3 tbsp chopped fresh parsley
pinch of celery salt
2 × 200 g/7 oz cans tuna fish in
    oil, drained
3 little gem lettuces
1 × 400 g/14 oz can flageolet
    beans, drained
1 × 400 g/14 oz can baby artichoke
    hearts, halved
12 cherry tomatoes, halved
toasted sesame bread, to serve

PREPARATION TIME

15 minutes

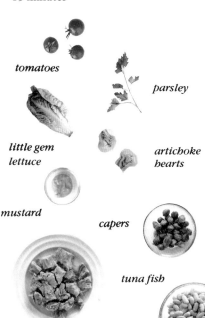

tomatoes

parsley

little gem lettuce

artichoke hearts

mustard

capers

tuna fish

flageolet beans

1 Combine the mayonnaise, mustard, capers and parsley in a mixing bowl. Season to taste with celery salt. Flake the tuna into the dressing and toss gently.

2 Arrange the lettuce leaves on four plates, then spoon the tuna mixture onto the leaves.

3 Spoon the flageolet beans to one side, followed by the tomatoes and artichoke hearts. Serve with slices of toasted sesame bread.

VARIATION

Flageolet beans are taken from the under-developed pods of haricot beans. They have a sweet creamy flavour and an attractive green colour. If not available, use white haricot or cannellini beans.

English Muffins with Sole, Spinach and Mushrooms

English muffins, frozen spinach and a few mushrooms form the beginning of this nourishing fish course. Any flatfish will do, although sole works best of all.

Serves 2

INGREDIENTS

115 g/4 oz/½ cup butter, plus extra
  for buttering muffins
1 medium onion, chopped
115 g/4 oz brown button mushrooms,
  sliced
2 fresh thyme sprigs, chopped
275 g/10 oz frozen leaf spinach,
  thawed
1.5 kg/3 lb sole or plaice to yield
  675 g/1½ lb skinned fillet
2 white English muffins, split
60 ml/4 tbsp crème fraîche
salt and freshly ground black pepper

<u>PREPARATION AND COOKING TIME</u>

20 minutes

English muffins

spinach

crème fraîche

thyme

sole

onion

1 Heat 50 g/2 oz/4 tbsp of the butter in a saucepan and add the onion. Cook over a gentle heat until soft but not coloured.

2 Add the mushrooms and thyme, cover and cook for a further 2–3 minutes. Remove the lid and increase the heat to drive off excess moisture.

3 Using the back of a large spoon, press the thawed frozen spinach in a sieve to extract the moisture.

4 Heat a further 25 g/1 oz/2 tbsp butter in a saucepan, add the spinach, heat through and season to taste.

5 Melt the remaining butter in a large frying pan, season the fillets and, with skin side uppermost, cook for 4 minutes, turning once.

COOK'S TIP
Approximately half of the weight of flatfish is bone, so if buying your fish whole, ask the fishmonger to give you the correct weight of boned fish.

6 Toast and butter the muffins. Divide the fillets between them, top with spinach and a layer of mushrooms, then finish with a spoonful of crème fraîche.

Dover Sole in a Green Parsley Jacket

Quick to prepare and absolutely delicious, nothing compares with the rich sweetness of a Dover sole. Here, this fine fish sports a green parsley jacket trimmed with lemon and a hint of garlic.

Serves 2

INGREDIENTS
350 g/12 oz floury potatoes, peeled and finely chopped
300 ml/½ pint/1¼ cups milk, or as required
pinch of grated nutmeg
2 × Dover sole, skinned
25 g/1 oz/2 tbsp butter
salt and freshly ground black pepper
lemon wedges, to serve

FOR THE PARSLEY JACKET
25 g/1 oz/½ cup fresh parsley
25 g/1 oz crustless white bread, cubed
45 ml/3 tbsp milk
30 ml/2 tbsp olive oil
finely grated zest of ½ small lemon
1 small garlic clove, crushed

PREPARATION AND COOKING TIME
15 minutes

Dover sole

lemon

parsley

1 In a non-stick saucepan, cover the potatoes with the milk, add salt to taste, and the nutmeg, and bring to the boil. Simmer, uncovered, for 15 minutes until the potatoes have absorbed the milk. Mash, cover and keep warm.

2 To make the parsley jacket, chop the parsley in a food processor. Add the bread, milk, olive oil, lemon zest and garlic, then reduce to a fine paste.

3 Preheat a moderate grill. Season the sole, dot with butter and grill for 5 minutes. Turn and allow 2 minutes on the other side. Spread with the parsley mixture, return to the grill and continue to cook for a further 5 minutes. Serve with the mashed potatoes and wedges of lemon.

VARIATION
The same parsley mixture can be used to cover fillets of cod, haddock, whiting or silver hake.

Salmon Risotto with Cucumber and Tarragon

Any rice can be used for risotto, although the creamiest ones are made with short-grain arborio and carnaroli rice. Fresh tarragon and cucumber combine well to bring out the flavour of the salmon.

Serves 4

INGREDIENTS

25 g/1 oz/2 tbsp butter
1 small bunch spring onions, white part only, chopped
½ cucumber, peeled, deseeded and chopped
400 g/14 oz/2 cups short-grain arborio or carnaroli rice
900 ml/1½ pints/3¾ cups chicken or fish stock
150 ml/¼ pint/⅔ cup dry white wine
450 g/1 lb salmon fillet, skinned and diced
45 ml/3 tbsp chopped fresh tarragon

PREPARATION AND COOKING TIME

20 minutes

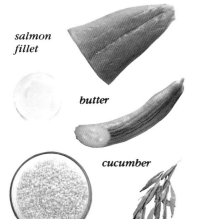

salmon fillet

butter

cucumber

rice

tarragon

spring onions

1 Heat the butter in a large saucepan, and add the spring onions and cucumber. Cook for 2–3 minutes without colouring.

2 Add the rice, stock and wine, return to the boil and simmer uncovered for 10 minutes, stirring occasionally.

3 Stir in the diced salmon and tarragon. Continue cooking for a further 5 minutes, then switch off the heat. Cover and leave to stand for 5 minutes before serving.

VARIATION

Long-grain rice can also be used. Choose grains that have not been pre-cooked and reduce the stock to 750 ml/1¼ pints/3⅔ cups, per 400 g/14 oz/2 cups of rice.

Grilled Snapper with Hot Mango Salsa

A ripe mango provides the basis for a deliciously rich fruity salsa. The dressing needs no oil and features the tropical flavours of coriander, ginger and chilli.

VARIATION

If fresh mangoes are unavailable, use the canned variety and drain well. Sea bream are also good served with the hot mango salsa.

Serves 4

INGREDIENTS
350 g/12 oz new potatoes
3 eggs
115 g/4 oz French beans, topped, tailed and halved
4 × 350 g/12 oz red snapper, scaled and gutted
30 ml/2 tbsp olive oil
175 g/6 oz mixed lettuce leaves, such as frisée or Webb's
2 cherry tomatoes
salt and freshly ground black pepper

FOR THE SALSA
45 ml/3 tbsp chopped fresh coriander
1 medium sized ripe mango, peeled, stoned and diced
½ red chilli, deseeded and chopped
2.5 cm/1 in fresh root ginger, grated
juice of 2 limes
generous pinch of celery salt

PREPARATION AND COOKING TIME
20 minutes

French beans

red snapper

mango

ginger

chilli

1 Bring the potatoes to the boil in a large saucepan of salted water and simmer for 15–20 minutes. Drain.

2 Bring a second large saucepan of salted water to the boil. Put in the eggs and boil for 4 minutes, then add the beans and cook for a further 6 minutes, so that the eggs have had a total of 10 minutes. Remove the eggs from the pan, cool, peel and cut into quarters.

3 Preheat a moderate grill. Slash each snapper three times on either side moisten with oil and cook for 12 minutes, turning once.

4 To make the dressing, place the coriander in a food processor. Add the mango, chilli, ginger, lime juice and celery salt and process smoothly.

5 Moisten the lettuce leaves with olive oil, and distribute them between four large plates.

6 Arrange the snapper over the lettuce and season to taste. Halve the new potatoes and tomatoes, and distribute them with the beans and quartered hard-boiled eggs over the salad. Serve with the salsa dressing.

Steaming Mussels with a Spicy Dipping Sauce

In this recipe, the mussel juices are thickened with split red lentils and spiced with curry.

Serves 4

INGREDIENTS
75 ml/5 tbsp red lentils
2 loaves French bread
1.8 kg/4 lb/4 pints live mussels
75 ml/5 tbsp white wine

FOR THE DIPPING SAUCE
30 ml/2 tbsp vegetable oil
1 small onion, finely chopped
½ celery stick, finely chopped
1 large garlic clove, crushed
5 ml/1 tsp medium-hot curry paste

PREPARATION TIME
5 minutes

COOKING TIME
15 minutes

curry paste

garlic

red lentils

French bread

onion

celery

mussels

1 Soak the lentils in plenty of cold water until they are required. Preheat the oven to 150°C/300°F/Gas 2 and put the bread in to warm. Clean the mussels in plenty of cold water and pull off any stray beards. Discard any that are damaged.

2 Place the mussels in a large saucepan. Add the white wine, cover and steam the mussels for 8 minutes. Discard any that do not open after cooking.

3 Transfer the mussels to a colander over a bowl to collect the juices. Keep warm until required.

4 To make the dipping sauce, heat the vegetable oil in a second saucepan, add the onion and celery, and cook for 3–4 minutes to soften without colouring. Strain the mussel juices into a measuring jug to remove any sand or grit. There will be approximately 425 ml/15 fl oz/ 1⅔ cups of liquid.

5 Add the mussel juices to the saucepan, then add the garlic, curry paste and lentils. Bring to the boil and simmer for 10–12 minutes or until the lentils have fallen apart.

6 Turn the mussels out onto four serving plates and bring to the table with the dipping sauce, the warm French bread and a bowl to put the empty shells in.

Grilled Sea Bream with Fennel, Mustard and Orange

Sea bream is a revelation to anyone unfamiliar with its creamy rich flavour. The fish has a firm white flesh that partners well with a rich butter sauce, sharpened here with a dash of frozen orange juice concentrate.

Serves 2

INGREDIENTS
2 jacket potatoes
2 × 350g/12 oz sea bream, scaled and gutted
10 ml/2 tsp Dijon mustard
5 ml/1 tsp fennel seeds
30 ml/2 tbsp olive oil
50 g/2 oz watercress
175 g/6 oz mixed lettuce leaves, such as curly endive or frisée

FOR THE SAUCE
30 ml/2 tbsp frozen orange juice concentrate
175 g/6 oz/¾ cup unsalted butter, diced
salt and cayenne pepper

PREPARATION AND COOKING TIME
20 minutes

Dijon mustard

orange juice

cayenne pepper

lettuce

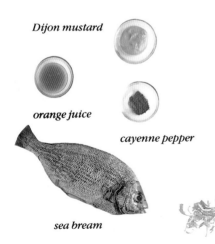

sea bream

COOK'S TIP

For speedy jacket potatoes, microwave small potatoes on 100% high power for 8 minutes, then crisp in a hot oven preheated to 200°C/400°F/Gas 6 for a further 10 minutes. Split, butter and serve.

1 Cook the potatoes according to the tip at the beginning of this recipe. Preheat a moderate grill. Slash the bream four times on either side. Combine the mustard and fennel seeds, then spread over both sides of the fish. Moisten with oil and grill for 12 minutes, turning once.

2 Place the orange juice concentrate in a bowl and heat over 2.5 cm/1 in of boiling water. Remove the pan from the stove, and gradually whisk the butter until creamy. Season, cover and set aside.

3 Moisten the watercress and lettuce leaves with the remaining olive oil, arrange the fish on two large plates and put the leaves to one side. Spoon over the sauce and serve with the potatoes.

Stir-fried Sweet and Sour Chicken

There are few cookery concepts that are better suited to today's busy lifestyle than the all-in-one stir-fry. This one has a South-east Asian influence.

Serves 4

INGREDIENTS
275 g/10 oz Chinese egg noodles
30 ml/2 tbsp vegetable oil
3 spring onions, chopped
1 garlic clove, crushed
2.5 cm/1 in fresh root ginger, peeled and grated
5 ml/1 tsp hot paprika
5 ml/1 tsp ground coriander
3 boneless chicken breasts, sliced
115 g/4 oz/1 cup sugar-snap peas, topped and tailed
115 g/4 oz baby sweetcorn, halved
225 g/8 oz fresh beansprouts
15 ml/1 tbsp cornflour
45 ml/3 tbsp soy sauce
45 ml/3 tbsp lemon juice
15 ml/1 tbsp sugar
45 ml/3 tbsp chopped fresh coriander or spring onion tops, to garnish

PREPARATION AND COOKING TIME
15 minutes

chicken breasts · garlic · spring onions · paprika · egg noodles · soy sauce · sugar-snap peas · ginger

COOK'S TIP
Large wok lids are cumbersome and can be difficult to store in a small kitchen. Consider placing a circle of greaseproof paper against the food surface to keep cooking juices in.

1 Bring a large saucepan of salted water to the boil. Add the noodles and cook according to the packet instructions. Drain, cover and keep warm.

2 Heat the oil. Add the spring onions and cook over a gentle heat. Mix in the next five ingredients, then stir-fry for 3–4 minutes. Add the next three ingredients and steam briefly. Add the noodles.

3 Combine the cornflour, soy sauce, lemon juice and sugar in a small bowl. Add to the wok and simmer briefly to thicken. Serve garnished with chopped coriander or spring onion tops.

Grilled Chicken with Pica de Gallo Salsa

This dish originates from Mexico. Its hot fruity flavours form the essence of Tex-Mex Cooking.

Serves 4

INGREDIENTS
4 chicken breasts
pinch of celery salt and cayenne
   pepper combined
30 ml/2 tbsp vegetable oil
corn chips, to serve

FOR THE SALSA
275 g/10 oz watermelon
175 g/6 oz canteloupe melon
1 small red onion
1–2 green chillies
30 ml/2 tbsp lime juice
60 ml/4 tbsp chopped fresh coriander
pinch of salt

PREPARATION TIME
5 minutes

COOKING TIME
15 minutes

green chillies

chicken breasts

red onion

lime

coriander

canteloupe melon

watermelon

COOK'S TIP
To capture the spirit of Tex-Mex food, cook the chicken over a barbecue and eat shaded from the hot summer sun.

1 Preheat a moderate grill. Slash the chicken breasts deeply to speed up the cooking time.

2 Season the chicken with celery salt and cayenne, brush with oil and grill for about 15 minutes.

3 To make the salsa, remove the rind and as many seeds as you can from the melons. Finely dice the flesh and put it into a bowl.

4 Finely chop the onion, split the chillies (discarding the seeds which contain most of the heat) and chop. Take care not to touch sensitive skin areas when handling cut chillies. Mix with the melon.

5 Add the lime juice and chopped coriander, and season with a pinch of salt. Turn the salsa into a small bowl.

6 Arrange the grilled chicken on a plate and serve with the salsa and a handful of corn chips.

Mexican Beef Burgers

Nothing beats the flavour and quality of a home-made burger. This version is from Mexico and is seasoned with cumin and fresh coriander.

Makes 4

INGREDIENTS
4 corn cobs
50 g/2 oz/1 cup stale white
    breadcrumbs
90 ml/6 tbsp milk
1 small onion, finely chopped
5 ml/1 tsp ground cumin
2.5 ml/½ tsp cayenne pepper
2.5 ml/½ tsp celery salt
45 ml/3 tbsp chopped fresh coriander
900 g/2 lb lean minced beef
4 sesame buns
60 ml/4 tbsp mayonnaise
4 tomato slices
½ iceberg lettuce or other leaves
    such as frisée or Webb's
salt and freshly ground black pepper
1 large packet corn chips,
    to serve

PREPARATION TIME
10 minutes

COOKING TIME
10 minutes

iceberg lettuce

minced beef

onion

tomatoes

sesame buns

white bread

1 Bring a large saucepan of water to the boil, add a good pinch of salt and cook the corn cobs for 15 minutes.

2 Combine the breadcrumbs, milk, onion, cumin, cayenne, celery salt and fresh coriander in a large bowl.

3 Add the beef and mix by hand until evenly blended.

4 Divide the mixture into four portions and flatten between sheets of clear film.

5 Preheat a moderate grill and cook for 10 minutes for medium burgers or 15 minutes for well-done burgers, turning once during the cooking time.

6 Split and toast the buns, spread with mayonnaise and sandwich the burgers with the tomato slices, lettuce leaves and seasoning. Serve with corn chips and the corn cobs.

COOK'S TIP

If planning ahead, freeze the burgers between sheets of greaseproof paper or clear film. Covered, they will keep well for up to twelve weeks. Defrost before cooking.

Black Pepper Beef Steaks with Red Wine Sauce

Every cook should know how to rustle up a pan-steak dinner with an impressive sauce to go with it. Black peppercorns follow the French tradition and combine well with the other bold flavours in the sauce.

Serves 4

INGREDIENTS
350 g/12 oz oven-ready chips or
　　4 jacket potatoes
15 ml/1 tbsp black peppercorns
4 × 225 g/8 oz sirloin or rump steaks
15 ml/1 tbsp olive oil
chopped fresh parsley, to garnish
150 g/5 oz green salad, to serve

FOR THE RED WINE SAUCE
120 ml/4 fl oz/½ cup red wine
75 g/3 oz dark open-cap mushrooms,
　　sliced
10 g/¼ oz dried morel mushrooms,
　　soaked (optional)
300 ml/½ pint/1¼ cups beef stock
15 ml/1 tbsp cornflour
5 ml/1 tsp Dijon mustard
2.5 ml/½ tsp anchovy essence
　　(optional)
10 ml/2 tsp red wine vinegar
25 g/1 oz/2 tbsp butter
salt and freshly ground black pepper

PREPARATION AND COOKING TIME
20 minutes

cornflour

mushrooms

anchovy essence

sirloin steaks

Dijon mustard

wine vinegar

peppercorns

1 Preheat the oven according to the instructions on the packet for oven-ready chips and cook. Alternatively, if you require jacket potatoes, cook in the microwave on high power (100%) for 8 minutes and then place in a preheated oven at 190°C/375°F/Gas 6 for a further 10 minutes. Crush the peppercorns using a pestle and mortar, or coarsely grind in a pepper mill. Coat both sides of the steak with the crushed peppercorns and brush lightly with olive oil.

2 Heat a heavy bare metal frying pan. Fry the steaks for 6–8 minutes for medium-rare or 12–16 minutes for well-done steaks, turning once throughout the cooking time.

3 Transfer the steaks to a plate, cover and keep warm. Pour off the excess fat from the frying pan, return to the heat and brown the sediment. To make the sauce, add the wine and stir with a flat wooden spoon to loosen the sediment.

4 Add the mushrooms to the frying pan with the dried morel, if using. Pour in the stock and cook briefly to soften.

5 Measure the cornflour, mustard and anchovy essence, if using, into a small bowl. Add 30 ml/2 tbsp of water and blend together to a smooth paste. Add to the frying pan, stirring continuously, and simmer to thicken.

COOK'S TIP

Non-stick frying pans are not suitable for making pan sauces. Only bare metal pans allow a rich sediment to form, which is essential to the flavour of a good sauce.

6 Add the vinegar to taste. Toss in the butter and swirl the contents in the pan with a circular motion until the butter has melted. Season to taste, return the steaks and heat through. Arrange the steaks on four plates, pour over the sauce and sprinkle with parsley. Serve with chips or baked potatoes and a green salad.

Lamb Chop Sauté with a Rich Pan Sauce

When lamb is sautéed in a heavy pan, a delicious sauce can be made from the sediment left behind.

Serves 4

INGREDIENTS

675 g/1½ lb new potatoes
4 × 175 g/6 oz lamb chops, chump,
  loin or leg steaks
15 ml/1 tbsp olive oil
3 fresh rosemary sprigs
75 ml/5 tbsp red wine
200 ml/7 fl oz/scant 1 cup chicken
  stock
10 ml/2 tsp cornflour
5 ml/1 tsp Dijon mustard
2.5 ml/½ tsp black olive paste
  (optional)
10 ml/2 tsp white wine vinegar
25 g/1 oz/2 tbsp unsalted butter
salt and freshly ground black pepper
carrots and petit pois, to serve

PREPARATION AND COOKING TIME

20 minutes

olive paste

lamb chops

Dijon mustard

red wine

black pepper

butter

rosemary

1 Bring the potatoes to the boil in a large saucepan of salted water and simmer for 15–20 minutes. Season the lamb with pepper and moisten with oil. Heat a large bare metal frying pan on the stove, add the rosemary and lay the meat over the top. Allow 6–8 minutes for medium-rare or 12–15 minutes for well-done lamb, turning once during the cooking time. Transfer to a warm plate, cover and allow the juices to settle.

2 Pour off any excess oil and discard the rosemary. Return the frying pan to the stove and heat the sediment until it browns. Add the wine and stir to loosen with a flat wooden spoon. Pour in the chicken stock and simmer.

3 Combine the cornflour, mustard and olive paste, if using, in a small bowl, adding 15 ml/1 tbsp of cold water to soften. Stir the contents of the bowl into the frying pan and simmer briefly to thicken. Add the vinegar, then stir in the butter. Arrange the potatoes, carrots, petit pois and lamb chops on four plates, pour over the sauce and serve.

Indonesian Pork and Peanut Saté

These delicious skewers of pork are popular street food in Indonesia. They are quick to make and eat.

Serves 4

INGREDIENTS
400 g/14 oz/2 cups long-grain rice
450 g/1 lb lean pork
pinch of salt
2 limes, quartered, to garnish
115 g/4 oz green salad, to serve

FOR THE BASTE AND DIP
15 ml/1 tbsp vegetable oil
1 small onion, chopped
1 garlic clove, crushed
2.5 ml/½ tsp hot chilli sauce
15 ml/1 tbsp sugar
30 ml/2 tbsp soy sauce
30 ml/2 tbsp lemon or lime juice
75 ml/5 tbsp water
2.5 ml/½ tsp anchovy essence
  (optional)
60 ml/4 tbsp smooth peanut butter

PREPARATION TIME
10 minutes

COOKING TIME
10 minutes

lemon

lime

rice

peanut butter

pork

garlic

chilli sauce

1 In a large saucepan, cover the rice with 900 ml/1 ½ pints/3¾ cups of boiling salted water, stir and simmer uncovered for 15 minutes until the liquid has been absorbed. Switch off the heat, cover and stand for 5 minutes. Slice the pork into thin strips, then thread zig-zag fashion onto 16 bamboo skewers.

2 Heat the vegetable oil in a pan. Add the onion and cook over a gentle heat to soften without colouring for about 3–4 minutes. Add the next 6 ingredients and the anchovy essence, if using. Simmer briefly, then stir in the peanut butter.

3 Preheat a moderate grill, spoon a third of the sauce over the pork and cook for 6–8 minutes, turning once. Spread the rice out onto a serving dish, place the pork saté on top and serve with the dipping sauce. Garnish with quartered limes and serve with a green salad.

VARIATION
Indonesian saté can be prepared with lean beef, chicken or prawns.

Pan-fried Pork with Peaches and Green Peppercorns

When peaches are in season, consider this speedy pork dish, brought alive with green peppercorns.

Serves 4

INGREDIENTS
400 g/14 oz/2 cups long-grain rice
1 litre/1¾ pints/4 cups chicken stock
4 × 200 g/7 oz pork chops or
    loin pieces
30 ml/2 tbsp vegetable oil
30 ml/2 tbsp dark rum or sherry
1 small onion, chopped
3 large ripe peaches
15 ml/1 tbsp green peppercorns
15 ml/1 tbsp white wine vinegar
salt and freshly ground black pepper

PREPARATION AND COOKING TIME

20 minutes

onion

pork chops

dark rum

oil

green peppercorns

white wine vinegar

peaches

VARIATION

If peaches are not ripe when picked, they can be difficult to peel. Only tree ripened fruit is suitable for peeling. If fresh peaches are out of season, a can of sliced peaches may be used instead.

1 Cover the rice with 900 ml/1½ pints/ 3¾ cups chicken stock. Stir, bring to a simmer and cook uncovered for 15 minutes. Switch off the heat and cover for 5 minutes. Season the pork with a generous twist of black pepper. Heat a large bare metal frying pan and moisten the pork with 15 ml/1 tbsp of the oil. Cook for 12 minutes, turning once.

2 Transfer the meat to a warm plate. Pour off the excess fat from the pan and return to the heat. Allow the sediment to sizzle and brown, add the rum or sherry and loosen the sediment with a flat wooden spoon. Pour the pan contents over the meat, cover and keep warm. Wipe the pan clean.

3 Heat the remaining vegetable oil in the pan and soften the onion over a steady heat.

4 Cover the peaches with boiling water to loosen the skins, then peel, slice and discard the stones.

5 Add the peaches and peppercorns to the onion and coat for 3–4 minutes, until they begin to soften.

6 Add the remaining chicken stock and simmer briefly. Return the pork and meat juices to the pan, sharpen with vinegar, and season to taste. Serve with the rice.

Sausage Popovers

This quick and filling dish is similar to Toad in the Hole, and is always well received.

Serves 4

INGREDIENTS
900 g/2 lb floury potatoes
450 g/1 lb pork or beef sausages or
 chipolatas
1 × 400 g/14 oz can petit pois, to
 serve (optional)

FOR THE BATTER
3 eggs
300 ml/½ pint/1¼ cups whole milk
115 g/4 oz/1 cup plain flour
salt and freshly ground black pepper

FOR THE ONION GRAVY
30 ml/2 tbsp vegetable oil
1 medium onion, chopped
15 ml/1 tbsp plain flour
200 ml/7 fl oz/scant 1 cup chicken or
 beef stock
5 ml/1 tsp balsamic or red
 wine vinegar

PREPARATION TIME
10 minutes

COOKING TIME
10 minutes

onion

eggs   *flour*

sausages

1 Cut the potatoes into small pieces to reduce the cooking time. Bring them to the boil in salted water and cook for 15 minutes. Preheat the oven to 230°C/450°F/Gas 8 and partly cook the sausages or chipolatas for 5 minutes.

2 To make the batter, beat the eggs together with a good pinch of salt and a twist of black pepper in a bowl.

3 Add half of the milk and all of the flour and stir into a smooth batter. Pour in the remaining milk and combine evenly.

4 Arrange the partly cooked sausages in a shallow muffin tray.

5 Pour in the batter, transfer to the preheated oven and bake for 10 minutes until well risen and golden.

COOK'S TIP

When making risen batter dishes, it is important to put the mixture into a fiercely hot oven.

6 To make the onion gravy, heat the vegetable oil in a large saucepan and brown the onion for 3–4 minutes, then add the flour. Remove from the heat, gradually stir in the stock and sharpen with vinegar to taste. Mash the potatoes and serve with the popovers, gravy and petit pois if desired.

Wild Mushroom Rösti with Bacon and Eggs

Dried ceps or porcini mushrooms, commonly found in Italian delicatessens, are a good substitute for fresh. Cook them in a potato rösti and serve with bacon and a fried egg for breakfast or a lazy supper.

Serves 4

INGREDIENTS
675 g/1½ lb floury potatoes, peeled
10 g/¼ oz dried ceps or porcini
    mushrooms
2 fresh thyme sprigs, chopped
30 ml/2 tbsp chopped fresh parsley
60 ml/4 tbsp vegetable oil, for frying
4 × 115 g/4 oz gammon or
    unsmoked bacon
pinch of salt
4 eggs, to serve
1 bunch watercress, to serve

PREPARATION AND COOKING TIME

20 minutes

bacon

thyme

parsley

potatoes

dried ceps

watercress

eggs

COOK'S TIP
A large rösti can be made in a non-stick frying pan. Allow 12 minutes to cook. Half-way through the cooking time, invert the rösti on a large plate and slide back into the pan.

1 Bring the potatoes to the boil in a large saucepan of salted water and cook for 5 minutes.

2 Cover the mushrooms with boiling water to soften, then chop roughly.

3 Drain the potatoes, allow them to cool and grate them coarsely. Add the mushrooms, thyme and parsley and combine together well.

4 Heat 30 ml/2 tbsp of the oil in a frying pan, spoon in the rösti mixture in heaps and flatten. Fry for 6 minutes, turning once during cooking.

5 Preheat a moderate grill and cook the gammon or bacon slices until they sizzle at the edges.

6 Heat the remaining oil in a frying pan and fry the eggs as you like them. Serve the rösti together with the eggs and bacon and a watercress salad.

Jambalaya

The perfect way to use up left-over cold meat –
Jambalaya is a fast, fortifying meal for a hungry family.

Serves 4

INGREDIENTS
45 ml/3 tbsp vegetable oil
1 medium onion, chopped
1 celery stick, chopped
½ red pepper, chopped
400 g/14 oz/2 cups long-grain rice
975 ml/1¾ pints/4 cups chicken
  stock
15 ml/1 tbsp tomato purée
3–4 shakes of Tabasco sauce
225 g/8 oz cold roast chicken or pork,
  thickly sliced
115 g/4 oz cooked sausage, such as
  chorizo or kabanos, sliced
75 g/3 oz/¾ cup frozen peas

PREPARATION AND COOKING TIME

20 minutes

roast chicken

peas

tomato purée

onion

sausages

celery   **red pepper**   **rice**

1 Heat the oil in a heavy saucepan and add the onion, celery and pepper Cook to soften without colouring.

2 Add the rice, chicken stock, tomato purée and Tabasco sauce. Simmer uncovered for 10 minutes.

3 Stir in the cold meat, sausage and peas and simmer for a further 5 minutes. Switch off the heat, cover and leave to stand for 5 minutes more before serving.

VARIATION

You could also add cooked ham, smoked cod or haddock and fresh shellfish to a Jambalaya.

Gorgonzola, Cauliflower and Walnut Gratin

This cauliflower dish is covered with a bubbly blue cheese sauce topped with chopped walnuts and cooked under the grill.

Serves 4

INGREDIENTS
1 large cauliflower, broken into florets
25 g/1 oz/2 tbsp butter
1 medium onion, finely chopped
45 ml/3 tbsp plain flour
450 ml/¾ pint/scant 2 cups milk
150 g/5 oz Gorgonzola or other blue cheese, cut into pieces
2.5 ml/½ tsp celery salt
pinch of cayenne papper
75 g/3 oz/¾ cup chopped walnuts
pinch of salt
fresh parsley, to garnish
115 g/4 oz green salad, to serve

PREPARATION TIME
10 minutes

COOKING TIME
10 minutes

onion

butter

 Gorgonzola — *walnuts*

cauliflower

1 Bring a large saucepan of salted water to the boil and cook the cauliflower for 6 minutes. Drain and place in a flameproof gratin dish.

2 Heat the butter in a heavy saucepan. Add the onion and cook over a gentle heat to soften without colouring. Stir in the flour, then draw from the heat. Stir in the milk a little at a time until absorbed by the flour, stirring continuously. Add the cheese, celery salt and cayenne pepper. Simmer and stir to thicken.

3 Preheat a moderate grill. Spoon the sauce over the cauliflower, scatter with chopped walnuts and grill until golden. Garnish with the parsley and serve with a crisp green salad.

VARIATION
For a delicious alternative, substitute cauliflower with 1.1 kg/2½ lb fresh broccoli or combine both together.

Risotto-stuffed Aubergines with Spicy Tomato Sauce

Aubergines are a challenge to the creative cook and allow for some unusual recipe ideas. Here, they are stuffed and baked with a cheese and pine nut topping.

Serves 4

INGREDIENTS
4 small aubergines
105 ml/7 tbsp olive oil
1 small onion, chopped
175 g/6 oz/scant 1 cup arborio rice
750 ml/1¼ pints/3⅔ cups
    vegetable stock
15 ml/1 tbsp white wine vinegar
8 fresh basil sprigs, to garnish

FOR THE TOPPING
25 g/1 oz/¼ cup freshly grated
    Parmesan cheese
15 g/½ oz/1 tbsp pine nuts

FOR THE TOMATO SAUCE
300 ml/½ pint/1¼ cups thick passata
    or tomato pulp
5 ml/1 tsp mild curry paste
pinch of salt

PREPARATION AND COOKING TIME
20 minutes

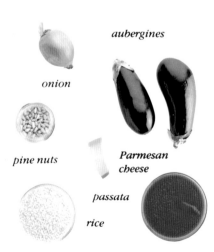

aubergines

onion

pine nuts

Parmesan cheese

passata

rice

COOK'S TIP

Don't be put off by the amount of oil aubergines absorb when cooking. Use olive oil and remember that good oils are low in saturated fat and are believed to fight against heart disease.

1 Preheat the oven to 200°C/400°F/Gas 6. Cut the aubergines in half lengthways and take out their flesh with a small knife. Brush with 30 ml/2 tbsp of the oil, place on a baking sheet and cook in the preheated oven for 6–8 minutes.

2 Chop the reserved aubergine flesh and heat the remainder of the olive oil in a medium saucepan. Add the aubergine flesh and the onion and cook over a gentle heat for 3–4 minutes until soft.

3 Add the rice, stir in the stock and simmer uncovered for a further 15 minutes. Stir in the vinegar.

4 Increase the oven temperature to 230°C/450°F/Gas 8. Spoon the rice into the aubergine skins, top with cheese and pine nuts, return to the oven and brown for 5 minutes.

5 To make the sauce, combine the passata or tomato pulp with the curry paste, heat through and add salt to taste.

6 Spoon the sauce onto four large serving plates and position two aubergine halves on each. Garnish with basil sprigs.

Spanish Omelette

Spanish omelette belongs in every cook's repertoire and can vary according to what you have in store. This version includes soft white beans and is finished with a layer of toasted sesame seeds.

VARIATION

You can also use sliced cooked potatoes, any seasonal vegetables, baby artichoke hearts and chick-peas in a Spanish omelette.

Serves 4

INGREDIENTS
30 ml/2 tbsp olive oil
5 ml/1 tsp sesame oil
1 Spanish onion, chopped
1 small red pepper, deseeded and diced
2 celery sticks, chopped
1 × 400 g/14 oz can soft white beans, drained
8 eggs
45 ml/3 tbsp sesame seeds
salt and freshly ground black pepper
115 g/4 oz green salad, to serve

PREPARATION TIME
10 minutes

COOKING TIME
10 minutes

celery

red pepper

white beans

sesame oil

sesame seeds

eggs

1 Heat the olive and sesame oils in a 30 cm/12 in paella or frying pan. Add the onion, pepper and celery and cook to soften without colouring.

2 Add the beans and continue to cook for several minutes to heat through.

3 In a small bowl beat the eggs with a fork, season well and pour over the ingredients in the pan.

4 Stir the egg mixture with a flat wooden spoon until it begins to stiffen, then allow to firm over a low heat for about 6–8 minutes.

5 Preheat a moderate grill. Sprinkle the omelette with sesame seeds and brown evenly under the grill.

6 Cut the omelette into thick wedges and serve warm with a green salad.

Omelette aux Fines Herbs

Eggs respond well to fast cooking and combine beautifully with a handful of fresh herbs. Serve with oven-ready chips and a green salad.

Serves 1

INGREDIENTS

3 eggs
30 ml/2 tbsp chopped fresh parsley
30 ml/2 tbsp chopped fresh chervil
30 ml/2 tbsp chopped fresh tarragon
15 ml/1 tbsp chopped fresh chives
15 ml/½ oz/1 tbsp butter
salt and freshly ground black pepper
350 g/12 oz oven-ready chips,
   to serve
115 g/4 oz green salad, to serve
1 tomato, to serve

PREPARATION AND COOKING TIME

15 minutes

eggs

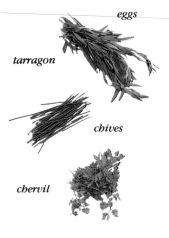

tarragon

chives

chervil

butter

parsley

1 Break the eggs into a bowl, season to taste and beat with a fork, then add the chopped herbs.

2 Heat an omelette or frying pan over a fierce heat, add the butter and cook until it foams and browns. Quickly pour in the beaten egg and stir briskly with the back of the fork. When the egg is two-thirds scrambled, let the omelette finish cooking for 10–15 seconds more.

3 Tap the handle of the omelette or frying pan sharply with your fist to make the omelette jump up the sides of the pan, fold and turn onto a plate. Serve with oven-ready chips, green salad and a halved tomato.

COOK'S TIP

From start to finish, an omelette should be cooked and on the table in less than a minute. For best results use free-range eggs at room temperature.

Macaroni Cheese with Mushrooms

Macaroni cheese is an all-time classic from the mid-week menu. Here it is served in a light creamy sauce with mushrooms and topped with pine nuts.

Serves 4

INGREDIENTS

450 g/1 lb quick-cooking elbow
    macaroni
45 ml/3 tbsp olive oil
225 g/8 oz button mushrooms, sliced
2 fresh thyme sprigs
60 ml/4 tbsp plain flour
1 vegetable stock cube
600 ml/1 pint/2½ cups milk
2.5 ml/½ tsp celery salt
5 ml/1 tsp Dijon mustard
175 g/6 oz/1½ cups grated
    Cheddar cheese
25 g/1 oz/¼ cup freshly grated
    Parmesan cheese
25 g/1 oz/2 tbsp pine nuts
salt and freshly ground black pepper

PREPARATION AND COOKING TIME

20 minutes

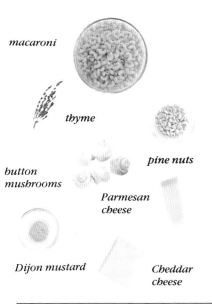

macaroni

thyme

pine nuts

button mushrooms

Parmesan cheese

Dijon mustard

Cheddar cheese

1 Bring a pan of salted water to the boil. Add the macaroni and cook according to the packet instructions.

2 Heat the oil in a heavy saucepan. Add the mushrooms and thyme, cover and cook over a gentle heat for 2–3 minutes. Stir in the flour and draw from the heat, add the stock cube and stir continuously until evenly blended. Add the milk a little at a time, stirring after each addition. Add the celery salt, mustard and Cheddar cheese and season. Stir and simmer briefly for 1–2 minutes until thickened.

3 Preheat a moderate grill. Drain the macaroni well, toss into the sauce and turn out into four individual dishes or one large flameproof gratin dish. Scatter with grated Parmesan cheese and pine nuts, then grill until brown and bubbly.

COOK'S TIP

Closed button mushrooms are best for white cream sauces. Open varieties can darken a pale sauce to an unattractive sludgy grey.

Red Pepper Polenta with Sunflower Salsa

This recipe is inspired by Italian and Mexican cookery. Cornmeal polenta is a staple food in Italy, served with brightly coloured vegetables. Mexican *Pipian* is made from sunflower seeds, chilli and lime.

Serves 4

INGREDIENTS
3 young courgettes
oil, for greasing
1.2 litres/2 pints/5 cups light
    vegetable stock
250 g/9 oz/2 cups fine polenta or
    cornmeal
1 × 200 g/7 oz can red peppers,
    drained and sliced
115 g/4 oz green salad, to serve

FOR THE SUNFLOWER SALSA
75 g/3 oz sunflower seeds, toasted
50 g/2 oz/1 cup crustless
    white bread
200 ml/7 fl oz/scant 1 cup
    vegetable stock
1 garlic clove, crushed
½ red chilli, deseeded and chopped
30 ml/2 tbsp chopped fresh coriander
5 ml/1 tsp sugar
15 ml/1 tbsp lime juice
pinch of salt

PREPARATION AND COOKING TIME

20 minutes

polenta

sunflower seeds

courgettes

limes

red chillies

red peppers

coriander

white bread

1 Bring a saucepan of salted water to the boil. Add the courgettes and simmer over a low heat for 2–3 minutes. Refresh under cold running water and drain. When they are cool, cut into strips.

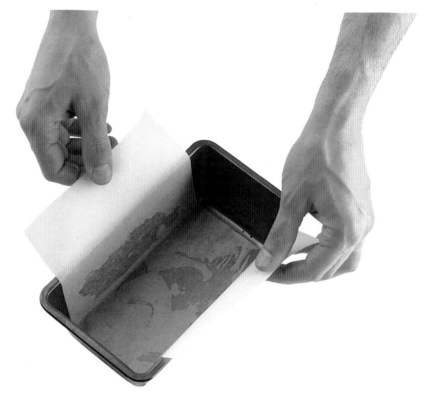

2 Lightly oil a 23 cm/9 in loaf tin and line with a single sheet of greaseproof paper.

3 Bring the vegetable stock to a simmer in a heavy saucepan. Add the polenta in a steady stream, stirring continuously for about 2–3 minutes until thickened.

4 Partly fill the lined tin with the polenta mixture. Layer the sliced courgettes and peppers over the polenta. Fill the tin with the remaining polenta and leave to set for about 10–15 minutes. Polenta should be served warm or at room temperature.

COOK'S TIP

Sunflower salsa will keep for up to 10 days in the refrigerator. It is delicious poured over a simple dish of pasta.

5 To make the salsa, reduce the sunflower seeds to a thick paste in a food processor. Add the remaining ingredients and combine thoroughly.

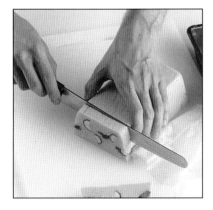

6 Turn the warm polenta out onto a board, remove the paper and cut into thick slices with a large wet knife. Serve with the salsa and a green salad.

Spinach and Ricotta Conchiglie

Large pasta shells are designed to hold a variety of delicious stuffings. Few are more pleasing than this mixture of chopped spinach and ricotta cheese.

Serves 4

INGREDIENTS
350 g/12 oz large conchiglie
450 ml/¾ pint/scant 2 cups passata or
    tomato pulp
275 g/10 oz frozen chopped spinach,
    defrosted
50 g/2 oz crustless white bread,
    crumbled
120 ml/4 fl oz/½ cup milk
45 ml/3 tbsp olive oil
250 g/8 oz/2¼ cups Ricotta cheese
pinch of nutmeg
1 garlic clove, crushed
15 ml/1 tbsp olive oil
2.5 ml/½ tsp black olive paste
    (optional)
25 g/1 oz/¼ cup freshly grated
    Parmesan cheese
25 g/1 oz/2 tbsp pine nuts
salt and freshly ground black pepper

PREPARATION AND COOKING TIME

20 minutes

olive paste

Ricotta cheese

pine nuts

garlic

spinach

conchiglie

COOK'S TIP
COOK'S TIP
Choose a large saucepan when cooking pasta and give it an occasional stir to prevent shapes from sticking together. If passata is not available, use a can of chopped tomatoes, sieved and puréed.

1 Bring a large saucepan of salted water to the boil. Toss in the pasta and cook according to the directions on the packet. Refresh under cold water, drain and reserve until needed.

2 Pour the passata or tomato pulp into a nylon sieve over a bowl and strain to thicken. Place the spinach in another sieve and press out any excess liquid with the back of a spoon.

3 Place the bread, milk and oil in a food processor and combine. Add the spinach and Ricotta and season with salt, pepper and nutmeg.

4 Combine the passata with the garlic, olive oil and olive paste if using. Spread the sauce evenly over the bottom of an ovenproof dish.

5 Spoon the spinach mixture into a piping bag fitted with a large plain nozzle and fill the pasta shapes (alternatively fill with a spoon). Arrange the pasta shapes over the sauce.

6 Preheat a moderate grill. Heat the pasta through in a microwave oven at high power (100%) for 4 minutes. Scatter with Parmesan cheese and pine nuts, and finish under the grill to brown the cheese.

Pasta Rapido with Parsley Pesto

Pasta suppers can often be dull. Here's a fresh, lively sauce that will stir the appetite.

Serves 4

INGREDIENTS
450 g/1 lb dried pasta
75 g/3 oz/¾ cup whole almonds
50 g/2 oz/½ cup flaked almonds, toasted
25 g/1 oz/¼ cup freshly grated Parmesan cheese
pinch of salt

FOR THE SAUCE
35 g/1½ oz fresh parsley
2 garlic cloves, crushed
45 ml/3 tbsp olive oil
45 ml/3 tbsp lemon juice
5 ml/1 tsp sugar
250 ml/8 fl oz/1 cup boiling water

PREPARATION AND COOKING TIME

20 minutes

pasta

lemon

parsley

garlic

Parmesan cheese

flaked almonds

almonds

1 Bring a large saucepan of salted water to the boil. Toss in the pasta and cook according to the instructions on the packet. Toast the whole and flaked almonds separately under a moderate grill until golden brown. Put the flaked almonds aside until required.

2 For the sauce, chop the parsley finely in a food processor. Add the whole almonds and reduce to a fine consistency. Add the garlic, olive oil, lemon juice, sugar and water. Combine to make a sauce.

COOK'S TIP
To prevent pasta from sticking together during cooking, use plenty of water and stir well before the water returns to the boil.

3 Drain the pasta and combine with half of the sauce. (The remainder of the sauce will keep in a screw-topped jar in the refrigerator for up to ten days.) Top with Parmesan and flaked almonds.

Succotash Soup Plate

Succotash is a North American Indian dish of corn and butter beans. Originally the dish was enriched with bear fat, although modern day succotash is finished with milk or cream. This version makes an appetizing and filling main course soup.

Serves 4

INGREDIENTS

50 g/2 oz/4 tbsp butter
1 large onion, chopped
2 large carrots, peeled and cut into
    short batons
900 ml/1½ pints/3¾ cups milk
1 vegetable stock cube
2 medium-sized waxy potatoes,
    peeled and diced
1 thyme sprig
225 g/8 oz/2 cups frozen sweetcorn
225 g/8 oz/3 cups frozen butter beans
    or broad beans
30 ml/2 tbsp chopped fresh parsley,
    to garnish

PREPARATION AND COOKING TIME

20 minutes

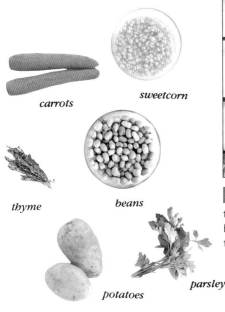

carrots

sweetcorn

thyme

beans

potatoes

parsley

1 Heat the butter in a large saucepan. Add the onion and carrots and cook over a gentle heat for 3–4 minutes, to soften without colouring.

2 Add the milk, stock cube, potatoes, thyme, sweetcorn and butter beans or broad beans. Simmer for 10 minutes until the potatoes are cooked through.

3 Season to taste, ladle into soup plates and garnish with chopped fresh parsley.

COOK'S TIP

Frozen sweetcorn and butter beans are best for flavour and convenience in this soup, although the canned variety may also be used.

Caponata

Caponata is a quintessential part of Sicilian antipasti and is a rich, spicy mixture of aubergine, tomatoes, capers and celery.

Serves 4

INGREDIENTS
60 ml/4 tbsp olive oil
1 large onion, sliced
2 celery sticks, sliced
450 g/1 lb aubergines, diced
5 ripe tomatoes, chopped
1 garlic clove, crushed
45 ml/3 tbsp red wine vinegar
15 ml/1 tbsp sugar
30 ml/2 tbsp capers
12 olives
pinch of salt
60 ml/4 tbsp chopped fresh parsley,
   to garnish
warm crusty bread, to serve
olives, to serve

PREPARATION TIME
10 minutes

COOKING TIME
10 minutes

celery

aubergines

onion   tomatoes

olives

capers

1 Heat half the oil in a large heavy saucepan. Add the onion and celery and cook over a gentle heat for about 3–4 minutes to soften.

2 Add the remainder of the oil with the aubergines and stir to absorb the oil. Cook until the aubergines begin to colour, then add the chopped tomatoes, garlic, vinegar and sugar.

3 Cover the surface of the vegetables with a circle of greaseproof paper and simmer for 8–10 minutes.

4 Add the capers and olives, then season to taste with salt. Turn the caponata out into a bowl, garnish with parsley and serve at room temperature with warm crusty bread and olives.

Red Berry Sponge Tart

When soft berry fruits are in season, try making this delicious sponge tart. Serve warm from the oven with scoops of vanilla ice cream.

Serves 4

INGREDIENTS

softened butter, for greasing
450 g/1 lb/4 cups soft berry fruits
   such as raspberries, blackberries,
   blackcurrants, redcurrants,
   strawberries or blueberries
2 eggs, at room temperature
50 g/2 oz/¼ cup caster sugar, plus
   extra to taste (optional)
15 ml/1 tbsp plain flour
50 g/2 oz/¾ cup ground almonds
vanilla ice cream, to serve

PREPARATION TIME

5 minutes

COOKING TIME

15 minutes

eggs

ground almonds

flour   *caster sugar*

redcurrants

lackcurrants

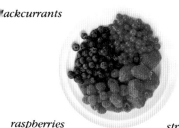

raspberries   *strawberries*

1 Preheat the oven to 190°C/375°F/ Gas 5. Brush a 23 cm/9 in flan tin with softened butter and line the bottom with a circle of non-stick baking paper. Scatter the fruit in the bottom of the tin with a little sugar if the fruits are tart.

2 Whisk the eggs and sugar together for about 3–4 minutes or until they leave a thick trail across the surface. Combine the flour and almonds, then fold into the egg mixture with a spatula – retaining as much air as possible.

3 Spread the mixture on top of the fruit base and bake in the preheated oven for 15 minutes. Turn out onto a serving plate and serve with vanilla ice cream.

VARIATION

When berry fruits are out of season, use bottled fruits, but ensure that they are well drained before use.

Raspberry and Passion Fruit Chinchillas

Few desserts are so strikingly easy to make as this one: beaten egg whites and sugar baked in a dish, turned out and served with a handful of soft fruit.

VARIATION

If raspberries are out of season, use either fresh, bottled or canned soft berry fruit such as strawberries, blueberries or redcurrants.

Serves 4

INGREDIENTS
25 g/1 oz/2 tbsp butter, softened
5 egg whites
150 g/5 oz/⅔ cup caster sugar
2 passion fruit
250 ml/8 fl oz/1 cup ready-made
    custard from a carton or can
milk, as required
675 g/1½ lb/6 cups fresh raspberries
icing sugar, for dusting

PREPARATION TIME
10 minutes

COOKING TIME
10 minutes

raspberries

egg whites

passion fruit

icing sugar

1 Preheat the oven to 180°C/350°F/ Gas 4. Brush four 300 ml/½ pint soufflé dishes with a visible layer of soft butter.

2 Whisk the egg whites in a mixing bowl until firm. (You can use an electric whisk.) Add the sugar a little at a time and whisk into a firm meringue.

3 Halve the passion fruit, take out the seeds with a spoon and fold them into the meringue.

4 Turn the meringue out into the prepared dishes, stand in a deep roasting pan which has been half-filled with boiling water and bake for 10 minutes. The meringue will rise above the tops of the soufflé dishes.

5 Turn the chinchillas out upside-down onto a serving plate. Thin the custard with a little milk and pour around the edge.

6 Top with raspberries, dredge with icing sugar and serve warm or cold.

Chocolate Mousse on the Loose

Super-light, dark, creamy and delicious; the chocolate mousse is always popular and should maintain a high profile on any dessert menu.

Serves 4

INGREDIENTS
200 g/7 oz best quality plain
    chocolate, plus extra for flaking
3 eggs
30 ml/2 tbsp dark rum or whisky
50 g/2 oz/¼ cup caster sugar
300 ml/½ pint/1¼ cups
    whipping cream
icing sugar, for dusting

PREPARATION TIME

15 minutes

plain chocolate

whipping cream

eggs

caster sugar

1 Break the chocolate into a bowl, stand over a saucepan of simmering water and melt. Separate the egg whites into a large mixing bowl, remove the chocolate from the heat and stir in the egg yolks and alcohol.

2 Whisk the egg whites until firm, gradually add the sugar and whisk until stiff peaks form.

3 Whip the cream to a dropping consistency and set aside until required.

4 Give the egg whites a final beating with a rubber spatula, add the chocolate and fold all the ingredients together gently, retaining as much air as possible.

5 Fold in the loosely whipped cream, turn into four glasses or bowls and chill until ready to serve.

COOK'S TIP

It is a false economy to use inexpensive chocolate. Choose the best quality dark chocolate you can find and enjoy it!

6 Decorate with flaked chocolate and dust with icing sugar.

Ice Cream Strawberry Shortcake

This pudding is an American classic, and couldn't be easier to make. Fresh juicy strawberries, store-bought flan cases and rich vanilla ice cream are all you need to create an irresistible feast of a dessert.

Serves 4

INGREDIENTS

3 × 15 cm/6 in sponge flan cases,
   or shortbreads
1.2 litres/2 pints/5 cups vanilla or
   strawberry ice cream
675 g/1½ lb hulled fresh strawberries
icing sugar, for dusting

PREPARATION TIME

10 minutes

strawberries

vanilla ice cream

flan case

1 If using flan cases, trim the raised edges with a serrated knife.

2 Sandwich the flan cases, or shortbreads with two-thirds of the ice cream and the strawberries.

3 Place the remaining ice cream on top, finish with strawberries, dust with icing sugar and serve.

COOK'S TIP

Don't worry if the shortbread falls apart when you cut into it. Messy cakes are best. Ice Cream Strawberry Shortbread can be assembled up to 1 hour in advance and kept in the freezer without spoiling the fruit.

Kentucky Fried Peaches

Never mind your diet, when peaches are this good, it's time for a break!

Serves 4

INGREDIENTS
5 large ripe peaches
50 g/2 oz/4 tbsp butter
30 ml/2 tbsp soft brown sugar
45 ml/3 tbsp Kentucky bourbon
1.2 litres/2 pints/5 cups vanilla
    ice cream
50 g/2 oz/½ cup pecan nuts, toasted

PREPARATION TIME
5 minutes

COOKING TIME
10 minutes

pecan nuts

vanilla ice cream

bourbon

peaches

butter

brown sugar

COOK'S TIP
Peaches that ripen after they are picked will not release their skins when blanched in boiling water.

1 Place the peaches in a large bowl and cover with boiling water to loosen their skins. Drain, refresh under cold running water and slice.

2 Heat the butter in a large frying pan until it foams and begins to brown. Add the sugar, peaches and bourbon, turn up the heat and cook until soft and syrupy. Spoon the hot peaches over the ice cream and decorate with pecan nuts.

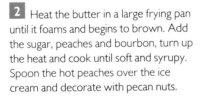

Apricot and Almond Bake

This dessert consists of a few apricots, either fresh or canned, strewn over an almond batter. Hot from the oven, this dessert is bound to please with a scoop or two of best vanilla ice cream.

COOK'S TIP

Metal pie plates are better than porcelain or pottery because they are better conductors of heat and will reduce the cooking time.

Serves 4

INGREDIENTS
50 g/2 oz/4 tbsp butter, softened, plus
    extra for greasing
50 g/2 oz/¼ cup caster sugar
50 g/2 oz/¾ ground almonds
15 ml/1 tbsp self-raising flour
1 egg
2.5 ml/½ tsp almond essence
175 g/6 oz/1 cup fresh apricots
    or 1 × 400 g/14 oz can apricots
    in syrup
icing sugar, for dusting
vanilla ice cream, custard or cream,
    to serve

PREPARATION TIME

10 minutes

COOKING TIME

10 minutes

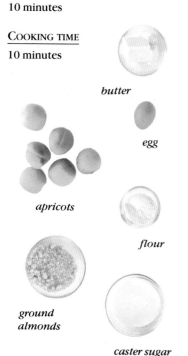

butter

egg

apricots

flour

*ground
almonds*

caster sugar

1 Preheat the oven to 200°C/400°F/ Gas 6. Lightly grease a 23 cm/9 in enamel pie plate with butter and set aside.

2 Soften the butter if necessary in a microwave oven for 20 seconds at 100% high power. Combine the butter and sugar in a mixing bowl.

3 Mix the ground almonds and flour together and add to the butter.

4 Add the egg and almond essence, then combine into a smooth batter.

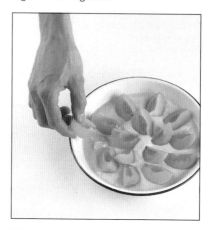

5 Turn the batter into a pie plate and spread it to the edge. Split the apricots, discard the stones if using fresh fruit, and arrange over the batter. Bake in the preheated oven for 15–20 minutes until springy to the touch.

6 Dust with icing sugar and serve hot with vanilla ice cream, cream or custard.

Black Forest Sundae

Here is a variation on the classic Black Forest Gâteau,
served in a sundae glass.

Serves 4

INGREDIENTS

1 × 400 g/14 oz stoned black
   cherries in syrup
15 ml/1 tbsp cornflour
45 ml/3 tbsp kirsch
150 ml/¼ pint/⅔ cup whipping
   cream
15 ml/1 tbsp icing sugar
600 ml/1 pint/2½ cups chocolate
   ice cream
115 g/4 oz chocolate cake
8 fresh cherries
vanilla ice cream, to serve

PREPARATION TIME

20 minutes

1 Strain all but 30 ml/2 tbsp of the cherry syrup into a saucepan. Measure the cornflour into a small bowl with the remaining syrup and combine.

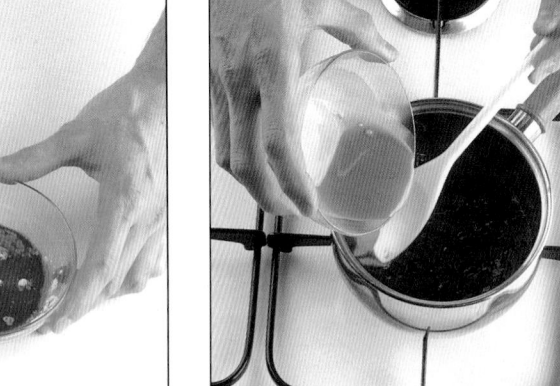

2 Bring the syrup in the saucepan to the boil. Stir in the cornflour and syrup mixture and simmer briefly to thicken.

3 Add the cherries, stir in the kirsch and spread onto a metal tray to cool.

chocolate ice cream

chocolate cake

black cherries

cherries

cornflour

whipping cream

4 Whip the cream with the icing sugar.

5 Place a spoonful of cherries in the bottom of four sundae glasses. Continue with layers of ice cream, chocolate cake, whipped cream and more cherries until the glasses are full.

COOK'S TIP

Bottled black cherries often have a better flavour than canned, especially if the stones are left in. You needn't remove the stones – just remember to warn your guests.

6 Finish with a piece of chocolate cake, two scoops of ice cream and more cream. Decorate with fresh cherries.

Chocolate Chip Banana Pancakes

Serve these delicious pancakes as a dessert topped with cream and toasted almonds.

Makes 16

INGREDIENTS
2 ripe bananas
200 ml/7 fl oz/scant 1 cup milk
2 eggs
150 g/5 oz/1¼ cups self-raising flour
25 g/1 oz/⅓ cup ground almonds
15 ml/1 tbsp caster sugar
25 g/1 oz plain chocolate chips
butter, for frying
pinch of salt

FOR THE TOPPING
150 ml/¼ pint/⅔ cup double cream
15 ml/1 tbsp icing sugar
50 g/2 oz/½ cup toasted flaked
almonds, to decorate

PREPARATION TIME
5 minutes

COOKING TIME
15 minutes

chocolate chips   *bananas*

eggs

flour

almonds

milk

1 In a bowl, mash the bananas with a fork, combine with half of the milk and beat in the eggs. Sieve in the flour, ground almonds, sugar and salt. Make a well in the centre and pour in the remaining milk. Add the chocolate chips and stir to produce a thick batter.

2 Heat a knob of butter in a non-stick frying pan. Spoon the pancake mixture into heaps, allowing room for them to spread. When bubbles emerge, turn the pancakes over and cook briefly on the other side.

3 Loosely whip the cream with the icing sugar to sweeten it slightly. Spoon the cream onto pancakes and decorate with flaked almonds.

COOK'S TIP

For banana and blueberry pancakes, replace the chocolate with 115 g/ 4 oz/1 cup fresh blueberries. Hot pancakes are also delicious when accompanied by ice cream.

Grilled Pineapple with Rum-custard Sauce

Freshly ground black pepper may seem an unusual ingredient to put with pineapple, until you realise that peppercorns are the fruit of a tropical vine. If the idea does not appeal, make the sauce without pepper.

Serves 4

INGREDIENTS
1 ripe pineapple
25 g/1 oz/2 tbsp butter
fresh strawberries, sliced, to serve

FOR THE SAUCE
1 egg
2 egg yolks
30 ml/2 tbsp caster sugar
30 ml/2 tbsp dark rum
2.5 ml/½ tsp freshly ground
   black pepper

PREPARATION TIME
10 minutes

COOKING TIME
5 minutes

butter

rum

eggs

pineapple

black pepper

caster sugar

1 Remove the top and bottom from the pineapple with a serrated knife. Pare away the outer skin from top to bottom, remove the core and cut into slices.

2 Preheat a moderate grill. Dot the pineapple slices with butter and grill for about 5 minutes.

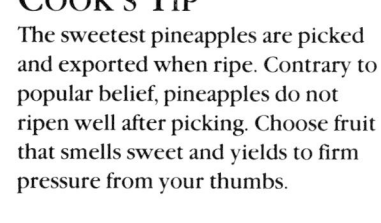

3 To make the sauce, place all the ingredients in a bowl. Set over a saucepan of simmering water and whisk with a hand-held mixer for about 3–4 minutes or until foamy and cooked. Scatter the strawberries over the pineapple and serve with the sauce.

COOK'S TIP
The sweetest pineapples are picked and exported when ripe. Contrary to popular belief, pineapples do not ripen well after picking. Choose fruit that smells sweet and yields to firm pressure from your thumbs.

Apples and Raspberries in Rose Pouchong Syrup

Inspiration for this dessert stems from the fact that the apple and the raspberry belong to the rose family. The subtle flavours are shared here in an infusion of rose-scented tea.

Serves 4

INGREDIENTS
5 ml/1 tsp rose pouchong tea
5 ml/1 tsp rose water (optional)
50 g/2 oz/¼ cup sugar
5 ml/1 tsp lemon juice
5 dessert apples
175 g/6 oz/1½ cups fresh raspberries

PREPARATION TIME
10 minutes

COOKING TIME
5 minutes

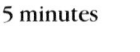
tea

apples

sugar

raspberries

COOK'S TIP
If fresh raspberries are out of season, use the same weight of frozen fruit or a 400 g/14 oz can of well drained fruit.

1 Warm a large tea pot. Add the rose pouchong tea and 900 ml/1½ pints/3¾ cups of boiling water together with the rose water, if using. Allow to stand and infuse for 4 minutes.

2 Measure the sugar and lemon juice into a stainless steel saucepan. Strain in the tea and stir to dissolve the sugar.

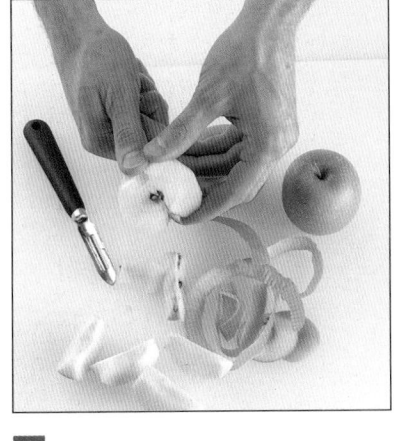

3 Peel and core the apples, then cut into quarters.

4 Poach the apples in the syrup for about 5 minutes.

5 Transfer the apples and syrup to a large metal tray and leave to cool to room temperature.

6 Pour the cooled apples and syrup into a bowl, add the raspberries and mix to combine. Spoon into individual dishes or bowls and serve warm.

INDEX